Y0-BTF-705

This book is dedicated to the many ladies, past and present, of the White Rock and South Surrey Newcomers' Club, and for their efforts to promote good fellowship among women.

The White Rock and South Surrey Newcomers' Club is organized to help women who are newcomers to our community feel welcome and provide them with an opportunity to become socially involved and knowledgeable about our community.

The Cook Book Committee would like to thank all the Newcomer and Alumni ladies who submitted recipes.

Cookbook Committee

| Vi Sakaki | Gretchen Hopkins | Sandy Taylor |
| Audrey Karpoff | Diana Sells | Lorraine Giordano |

This cookbook was typeset, printed and bound by

Rasmussen Company

"The Cookbook Printer"

111 Plymouth Street
Winnipeg, Manitoba R2X 2V5

Phone or write for free information
on getting a fund raising cookbook printed
for your school, church, community organization, etc.

Phone Toll Free 1-800-665-0222

Visit our website at
www.cookbookprinter.com

We would like to thank all the businesses and individuals who have given their valuable support to our organization.

We gratefully acknowledge the continued support of the following sponsors -

Bay Wines
Boardwalk Optometry
Carol Swaykoski CTC - Village Travel & Cruises
Cielo's Restaurant
Curran's Lingerie
Dr. Robert Holden, Chiropractor
Dr. William Liang Dental Care
Enchanted Harvest Florist & Home Decor
Garden Works
Gasland Equipment & Fireplaces Inc.
Giovanni Jewellers Ltd.
Giraffe Restaurant
Gord Murray - Sutton Group - West Coast Realty
Hershey Canada, BC District
HSBC - South Point Exchange
I Do Bridal Inc.
Iguana's Beach Grill
Island Blends Coffee House - South Point Annex
Japan Bonsai Garden Art
Jonker Nissan
Kiki's Restaurant
Liberty Wine Merchants - South Point Exchange
Lois Wilson - Homelife Benchmark Realty
Magique Ladies Fashion Boutique
Mike Mahaffey - Homestead Contracting
Nathan Construction Ltd.
Never E'nuff Clothes - Ocean Park & Peninsula Village
Peace Arch Toyota
Ranka Burzan - Clean & Tidy Solutions
Richard Walter Investment Group
Salon Montage
Save On Foods - South Point Exchange
Scotiabank - Redwood Square
Scruples Quality Consignment Wear
Sundance Buffalo
Toscana Home & Garden Decor
Wolfie's Restaurant

NOTES

Contents

(ID#14674)

My Favourite Recipes

Name of Recipe	Page #

Appetizers
& Beverages

COOKING TERMS

Bake — To cook by dry heat, either covered or uncovered, in an oven or oven-type appliance.

Baste — To moisten meat or other foods with pan drippings, fruit juice or a sauce. Prevents drying of food surface and adds flavor.

Beat — To make a mixture smooth by introducing air with a brisk over and over motion using a spoon, or a rotary motion using an egg beater or electric mixer.

Blanch — To preheat in boiling water or steam. Helps loosen skins of fruits, vegetables or nuts; also used to prepare food for canning, freezing or drying.

Blend — To combine two or more ingredients thoroughly.

Boil — To heat a liquid until bubbles continuously break on the surface.

Braise — To cook slowly in a small amount of liquid in a covered pan.

Bread — To coat with flour, then dip into slightly diluted beaten egg or milk, and finally coat with bread, cereal or cracker crumbs.

Broil — To cook by direct heat, under a broiler or over hot coals.

Caramelize — To melt sugar, or foods containing sugar, slowly over low heat without burning, until it melts and becomes brown in color.

Chop — To cut food into small pieces with a knife.

Clarify — To make a liquid (stock, broth, butter) clear by skimming away or filtering out fat or other impurities.

Coat — To cover food evenly with flour, crumbs or batter.

Coddle — To cook food slowly in water just below the boiling point.

Compote — Fruit stewed or cooked in syrup, usually served as a dessert.

Cool — To let food stand at room temperature until it is no longer warm to the touch.

Cream — To make a fat, such as butter, soft and smooth by beating with a spoon or mixer. Also, to combine a fat with sugar until mixture is light and fluffy.

Cube — To cut a solid food into cubes of about ½ inch or more.

Cut in — To mix evenly a solid fat into dry ingredients (e.g. shortening and flour) by chopping with two knives or a pastry blender.

Dice — To make small cubes of ⅛ to ¼ inch.

Dredge — To cover or coat food with flour or a similar fine, dry substance.

Dust — To sprinkle lightly with flour or sugar.

Fillet — A piece of meat, poultry or fish without bones.

Flake — To break food into small pieces, usually with a fork.

Flute — To make decorative indentations around edge of pastries, fruits or vegetables.

Fold — To combine two ingredients. Using a spoon or rubber spatula, go down through the mixture on the far side of the bowl, bring the spoon across the bottom of the bowl and up the near side, turn the mixture over on the top. Turn bowl slightly and repeat till mixture is blended.

Fry — To cook in hot fat; pan-fry or sauté in a small amount of fat, deep-fat fry in deep layer of fat that covers the food.

Glaze — To coat with a smooth mixture to give food a glossy appearance.

Grate — To rub food against a grater to form small particles.

Grill — To cook on a rack over hot coals or other direct heat.

Grind — To reduce to particles in a grinder, blender or food processor.

Julienne — To cut meat, vegetables or fruit into long matchlike strips.

Knead — To manipulate with a pressing motion accompanied by folding and stretching. For yeast bread: fold dough toward you, push dough away using the heel of your hand. Rotate ¼ turn and repeat. For tea biscuits: kneading process is much less vigorous and requires less time.

Marinate — To let food stand in a seasoned sauce called a **marinade** to tenderize and increase flavor.

Mince — To cut or chop into very small pieces, but smaller than diced.

Mix — To combine ingredients until evenly distributed.

Panbroil — To cook uncovered on a hot surface removing fat as it accumulates.

Parboil — To cook food in a boiling liquid until partially done. Cooking is usually completed by another method.

Pare — To remove outer covering of fruit or vegetable with a knife.

Peel — To strip off or pull away outer covering of fruit or vegetable.

Poach — To cook slowly in simmering liquid such as water or milk.

Purée — To put food through a sieve, blender or processor to produce the thick pulp or paste with juice.

Reduce — To rapidly boil down the volume of a liquid to concentrate flavor.

Roast — To cook meat in an uncovered pan by dry heat in an oven.

Sauté — To brown or cook in a small amount of fat (see **fry**).

Scald — To heat milk to just below the boiling point, when tiny bubbles appear around the edge of the pan; to dip certain foods briefly into boiling water (see **blanch**).

Score — To make shallow slits into the surface of a food in a diamond or rectangular pattern.

Sear — To brown and seal surface of meat quickly with intense heat.

Shred — To cut into long, thin strips with a knife or shredder.

Simmer — To cook in liquid just below boiling point; bubbles form slowly and burst before reaching surface.

Sliver — To cut into long thin pieces with a knife; e.g. almonds, or pimiento.

Steam — To cook in a covered container above boiling water.

Steep — To let stand for a few minutes in water that has just been boiled to enhance flavor and color.

Stew — To simmer slowly in liquid deep enough to cover.

Stir — To mix ingredients in a circular motion until blended with uniform consistency.

Stir fry — To cook in a frypan or wok over high heat in a small amount of fat, tossing or stirring constantly.

Toast — To brown with dry heat in an oven or toaster.

Whip — To beat rapidly with a wire whisk, beater or mixer to incorporate air to lighten and increase volume.

APPETIZERS & BEVERAGES

GRILLED BRIE AND FRUIT CROSTINI   *Olga Langevin*

Fruit Salsa:
1/2 cup diced mango
1/2 cup diced red apple, with
  peel
1/2 cup white kidney beans,
  drained, rinsed and coarsely
  chopped
2 Tbsp finely chopped red
  onion
1 small hot pepper, seeded and
  diced very fine (optional)

2 Tbsp balsamic vinegar
2 tsp granulated sugar
1 Tbsp chopped fresh parsley
1 Tbsp chopped fresh cilantro
24 baguette slices, cut 1/2 inch
  thick
2 (4 oz) small Brie cheese
  rounds with rind
1/4 cup olive oil

For the fruit salsa, combine first 9 ingredients in a bowl. Cover. Let stand at room temperature for 1 hour, stirring several times, for flavours to meld. Makes 2 cups salsa.

Preheat, lightly sprayed electric grill, to medium 350°F heat. Lightly brush baguette slices and Brie rounds on both sides with olive oil. Place baguette slices on grill. Cook for about 1 minute until toasted on both sides. Increase heat to medium-high. Place both Brie rounds on grill. Cook for 4 to 5 minutes on each side, turning carefully, until soft to touch. Serve with salsa. Makes 24 appetizer servings.

BRIE FONDUE   *Lorraine Giordano*

1/4 stick butter
4 shallots, peeled and chopped
2 Tbsp flour
1 1/2 cups chicken broth
2 cups ripe Brie

2/3 cup whipping cream
2 Tbsp lemon juice
1 tsp paprika
1 Tbsp freshly chopped parsley
Dash Tabasco sauce

Melt butter in fondue pot and sauté shallots for 10 minutes. Add flour and heat for 2 minutes. Gradually add broth and simmer for approximately 5 minutes. Discard rind from Brie and cube. Add Brie and whipping cream to the broth mixture. Stir until smooth. Add lemon juice. Add other spices.

RACLETTE CRISPS
WITH PECANS AND BASIL
Kathryn Waldie

1/2 lb Raclette cheese
1/4 cup chopped pecans

8 leaves fresh basil, roughly
chopped

Preheat oven to 350°F. Slice the cheese into pieces 1 1/2 inch round and 1/4 inch thick. Place the pieces 2 inches apart on a nonstick cookie sheet, or a cookie sheet lined with parchment paper (you must allow the cheese to spread as it melts). Sprinkle each piece of cheese with some of the pecans and basil. Bake for 10 to 15 minutes or until the oil bubbles from the cheese; if you let the cheese become brown, it will be bitter. Cool the crisps on the cookie sheet and remove with a metal spatula. Serve at room temperature.

PATE MAISON
Dorothy Cunningham

3 medium onions, sliced 1/4
   inch thick
8 oz butter, divided
2 lb chicken livers, washed and
   drained

3 cloves garlic, chopped
1/2 tsp dried thyme
1 bay leaf
3 oz brandy

Fry onions in 2 ounces of butter in a large skillet. When browned nicely, add livers, and mix. Add garlic, bay leaf and thyme and cook for 45 minutes over medium heat, stirring frequently until livers are cooked through. Remove from heat and cool. Remove bay leaf, and process to a fine texture. Mix in remaining butter. Salt and pepper to taste. Add the brandy. Mix well. Store in sterile pots in the refrigerator or freeze. Thaw at room temperature. Serve with crackers.

SUNDANCE SALMON PATE
Sandy Taylor

4 oz smoked salmon
4 oz cream cheese
1 Tbsp chopped red onion

1/2 tsp chopped garlic
1 pinch fresh parsley
1 tsp lemon juice

Drain smoked salmon. Put all ingredients into a food processor or blender and mix until well blended. Put into serving bowl and chill for 30 minutes. Serve with baguettes or crackers.

SMOKED TROUT PATE

12 oz smoked trout	1 Tbsp horseradish sauce
2 oz butter, softened	1 Tbsp lemon juice
4 oz cream cheese	Pepper, to taste
2 Tbsp soured cream	Paprika to garnish

Flake the fish into a bowl. Beat together butter and cream cheese until soft. Beat in soured cream, horseradish sauce and lemon juice. Stir in flaked fish and season with pepper. Spoon into a serving dish and sprinkle paprika pepper on top and leave to chill. Alternatively, place all the ingredients into a food processor and blend for approximately 1 minute.

COCONUT SHRIMP LOLLYPOPS   *Dorinda Torrance*

Large raw shrimps, shelled and tails removed	1/2 to 1 tsp cayenne pepper
Seafood batter mix, made up according to pkg directions	Long shredded coconut

Curl shrimp into circles and hold with wooden toothpick. Dip into batter. Roll in long shred coconut. Drop into very hot vegetable oil and fry for approximately 1 minute per side. Cool on parchment paper. When cooked, place on paper towel to remove some of the oil.

COCONUT SHRIMP   *Maureen Cockburn*

1 lb large shrimp, peeled and deveined	1 1/2 cups dried grated coconut
Batter:	1 Tbsp salt
3/4 cup flour	1/2 Tbsp pepper
1 egg	1/2 Tbsp cayenne
1/2 tsp baking powder	1/2 Tbsp paprika
1/2 cup beer	1 Tbsp garlic powder
Coating:	1/2 tsp thyme
1/4 cup flour	1/2 tsp oregano

Dip each shrimp in batter and then roll in the coating. Deep fry until batter cooked. Drain on paper towels. Serve with dips.

CRAB DIP
Gretchen Hopkins

6 oz can crab meat
1/2 cup sour cream
1/4 cup mayonnaise
1 Tbsp chopped onion

1 tsp horseradish
1 Tbsp parsley
1 tsp mustard
Dash Tabasco

Mix and chill for 2 hours.

ARTICHOKE TOASTIES
Dorinda Torrance

12 slices white sandwich bread
Soft butter for spreading
14 oz can artichoke hearts,
   drained and chopped
2 oz fresh Parmesan cheese,
   finely grated

2 fresh, fleshy, mild green
   chiles, seeded and finely
   chopped
3 heaping Tbsp mayonnaise
Pinch salt
Freshly ground black pepper

Using a cookie cutter, cut two circles of bread out of each slice of bread. Butter one side fairly generously and press butter-side down in a shallow nonstick muffin pan, flattening the entire surface with your fingertips. Mix together the remaining ingredients, then place a spoonful of the mixture into each bread case, smoothing down the top evenly. Bake in the preheated oven at 425°F for 12 to 15 minutes, until golden and crisp. Let cool briefly before slipping out of the pan. Yield: 24.

HOT ARTICHOKE DIP
Inger-Lise Koetke

14 oz can artichoke hearts,
   drained and chopped
1/2 cup Parmesan cheese
   (freshly grated is best)

1 cup mayonnaise
1/2 tsp garlic salt
Dash lemon juice

Mix all ingredients together. Heat in oven at 350°F for 10 minutes. Serve with crackers.

GRINGOS' GUACAMOLE
Simone Mackenzie

2 to 3 ripe avocados
2 cloves garlic, crushed
Dash lemon juice

1 tsp Tabasco sauce (more if
   you like it hotter)
Salt to season

Put the avocados in a bowl and mash with a fork. Add the rest of the ingredients and serve with hot pita bread or crackers.

TEX MEX DIP

Margaret Roller

3 medium ripe avocados, peel, pit and mash
2 Tbsp lemon juice
1/2 tsp salt
1/4 tsp pepper
1 cup sour cream
1/2 cup mayonnaise
1 pkg taco mix seasoning
1 to 2 cans refried beans
1 small bunch green onions, chopped
3 medium tomatoes, chopped
1 cup pitted ripe black olives, drained and chopped
8 oz grated sharp cheddar cheese

Peel, pit and mash avocados. Add to this lemon juice, salt and pepper. In a separate bowl mix sour cream, mayonnaise and taco mix seasoning. Spread refried beans in a shallow serving dish. Top with avocado mixture and top this with sour cream mixture. Sprinkle remaining items on top. Cover with plastic wrap and refrigerate for a few hours. Serve chilled with tortilla chips. Serves 12 to 15.

OLD ENGLISH PUB DIP

Dorothy Cunningham

250 g pkg cream cheese, softened
1/4 cup soft butter
250 g pkg soft Imperial cheddar cheese
1 tsp Worcestershire sauce
1 tsp horseradish
2 to 3 drops Tabasco (more or less to taste)
1/4 tsp pepper
1/2 tsp crushed garlic (more or less to taste)
1/4 cup beer (more if needed, but thickens as it chills)

Blend all ingredients together in processor until smooth. Pack in clean ceramic or glass pots, refrigerate. This will freeze well in small pots. Thaw at room temperature. Serve with crackers, garnished with chopped nuts and paprika.

*Opportunity: a good chance that
always looks bigger going than coming.*

ANTIPASTO

Joan McFarlane

3 medium sized carrots
1 cauliflower
3 (14 oz) cans black olives, drained
14 oz can green olives, drained
14 oz jar sour white onions, drained
14 oz can green beans, drained

6 green peppers, cleaned and roughly chopped
6 red peppers, cleaned and roughly chopped
2 (10 oz) cans mushrooms
1 small jar sliced pimento
1 cup olive oil
1/2 cup white vinegar
50 oz ketchup

Cut up the carrots and cauliflower (not too small) and steam or boil slightly for 1 minute. Combine all the other ingredients and boil for 10 minutes. Fill jars to almost full and boil for 25 to 30 minutes in canner. This recipe makes about 12 (250 mL) jars or you can use 125 mL jars. Prepare jars and have canning pot ready for use.

HOT AND CREAMY SWISS ALMOND SPREAD

Cathy Guarasci

250 g pkg light cream cheese, softened
1 1/2 cups grated Swiss cheese

1/3 cup Miracle Whip light dressing
1/3 cup sliced almonds, toasted
2 Tbsp chopped green onions

Heat oven to 350°F. Combine all ingredients, mix well. Spoon mixture into a deep 2 cup oven proof casserole dish. Bake for 15 minutes, stirring after 8 minutes. Serve warm with vegetables and crackers. Garnish with toasted, sliced almonds if desired. Makes 1 1/2 cups.

FETA PINE NUT SPREAD

Diane Schachter

1/3 cup drained sun-dried tomatoes
3 Tbsp toasted pine nuts
1 garlic clove

2 Tbsp chopped basil or 2 tsp dried basil
1 tsp lemon juice
8 oz cream cheese
7 oz feta cheese

Combine tomatoes, nuts, garlic, basil, and lemon juice in blender and blend until mixed and chopped. Add cream and feta cheese. Blend until combined but still chunky. Serve with crackers, apples or bagels.

MID-EASTERN FLAVOURED CHEESE APPETIZER

Marilyn Brown

250 g pkg cream cheese
1 tsp curry powder
1/4 tsp turmeric
1/4 cup red pepper jelly (e.g. Red Chili Delight, found in deli sections)

1/4 cup English or Major Grey chutney
Pine nuts as required
Green onions, chopped as needed
Currants, as needed

The night before, mix cheese, curry powder, and turmeric together so the flavours can blend. Next day, form cheese into round disc, then roll or press pine nuts onto the top and sides. Before serving mix the jelly and the chutney together and spread over the cheese ball. Sprinkle with green onions, then the currants on top. Serve surrounded with water crackers.

MANGO CHUTNEY APPY

Betty Bishop

8 oz cream cheese
1 tsp curry
2 tsp cumin
2 Tbsp mango chutney
Jalapeno pepper jelly

Dried cranberries and/or currants
Chopped onions
Pine nuts and/or almonds

Process first four ingredients and spread in a dish. Spread jalapeno pepper jelly on top and then spread the layer of cranberries, onions and nuts on top of jelly.

TINY PIZZAS

Norma Mills

1 cup cheddar cheese, shredded
1/2 cup vegetable oil
4 oz can tomato sauce
1 small can red pimentos, drained and chopped

1 small can green olives, chopped
1 can mushrooms, chopped
Salt, pepper and garlic, to taste
1 slim French stick

Mix all the ingredients, except bread, together. Cut French stick in 1/2 to 3/4 inch slices and spread mixture on each slice. Broil until bubbly. Remove from heat and serve.

QUICHE - MINI TARTS

Maureen Cockburn

1/2 cup grated old cheese
8 eggs, beaten
1 green pepper, chopped
6 green onions, chopped

1 cup chopped broccoli
8 oz ham, chopped
16 Ritz biscuits, crushed
8 oz mushrooms, chopped

Mix all ingredients together and bake in mini tart pan sprayed with Pam for 20 minutes at 375°F.

VEGETABLE CRESCENT ROLLS

Alyson Clifton

2 pkg crescent rolls
1 pkg Knorr vegetable soup
  mix
1/2 cup mayonnaise
1/2 cup sour cream
1 pkg frozen chopped spinach,
  thawed and drained

1 can artichoke hearts in water,
  drained
1 can water chestnuts, drained
  and chopped
4 oz feta cheese
2 cloves garlic
Parmesan cheese

Spread crescent roll pastry on a cookie tray and roll out to edges and up sides. Bake at 375°F for 10 to 12 minutes. Meanwhile mix all other ingredients, except Parmesan, together in a large bowl. Spread this mixture on pastry and sprinkle with Parmesan cheese. Bake at 375°F for 10 minutes.

CHEESY SALMON PINWHEELS

Sandy Taylor

1 container vegetable flavored
  cream cheese
3 Tbsp grated Parmesan
  cheese
2 Tbsp minced fresh chives

1 tsp milk or cream
1/2 tsp freshly ground pepper
4 (10 inch/25.5 cm) diameter
  flour tortillas
9 oz smoked salmon lox

In a small mixing bowl, combine cheese, chives, milk and pepper. Spread mixture evenly on tortillas. Arrange salmon slices evenly over cheese mixture. Roll up tortillas to enclose fillings. Wrap in plastic wrap, and chill for at least 1 hour. Trim ends of tortilla rolls. Cut each roll into nine pinwheels about 1/2 inch thick.

HAM PASTIES

Maureen Cockburn

Pastry:
5 cups Robin Hood all purpose flour (regular or instant blending)
1 Tbsp brown sugar
1 tsp salt
1/2 tsp baking powder
1 lb lard
3/4 cup cold water
1 egg
2 tsp vinegar
1 egg
1 Tbsp water
Poppy seeds, caraway seeds or sesame seeds

Filling:
3 cups finely diced (1/4 inch) cooked ham
2 Tbsp chopped green pepper
2 Tbsp chopped pimento
1 Tbsp minced onion
10 1/2 oz can undiluted, condensed cream of mushroom soup

Measure unsifted flour into large mixing bowl. Add brown sugar, salt and baking powder; stir well to blend. Add half the lard and rub in with fingertips. Cut the remaining lard until particles are the size of small peas. Combine water, egg and vinegar in small bowl. Beat slightly. Add all at once to flour mixture and stir with fork until dough holds together. Form into a ball and wrap in waxed paper. Chill before using. Roll out portions of the dough on lightly floured surface for 1/8 inch thickness. Cut into circles using 3 1/4 or 4 inch cutter. Place circles on ungreased baking sheets.

Combine all filling ingredients, mixing well. Spread a scant tablespoon of filling on one half of pastry. Moisten edge and fold over. Seal edges with tines of a fork. Cut slits in tops of pasties for steam to escape. Brush pasties with mixture of 1 egg beaten and 1 tablespoon of water. Sprinkle poppy seeds, caraway seeds or sesame seeds over top if desired. Bake at 400°F for 15 to 20 minutes or until golden brown. Serve warm. Yield: 4 1/2 dozen.

Pasties may be baked and frozen, to be reheated before serving; or they may be frozen unbaked. Pastry dough will keep several weeks in the refrigerator and is excellent for pies. Will make 2 double crust pies and 1 pie shell.

What you don't know won't help you much either.

MUSHROOM ROLLS

Wendy Ternowesky

1/4 cup margarine or butter
1/2 cup onion, chopped
1/2 lb mushrooms
1/2 tsp Worcestershire sauce
1/2 tsp salt
1/8 tsp pepper

1/8 tsp garlic powder
250 g cream cheese
1 loaf white bread, sliced thin
1/4 cup melted margarine or
butter

Fry chopped onion and mushrooms in melted butter until soft. Drain off some of the liquid. Add remaining spices. Stir in cream cheese and heat until melted. Cool. Remove crusts from the loaf of bread. Roll each slice until flat. Spread mixture on bread and roll up. Brush melted margarine on each piece. Freeze. Cut into thirds. Bake on ungreased cookie sheet in 400°F oven for 12 to 15 minutes. Makes approximately 4 dozen.

WON TON TARTS

Lorraine Giordano

1 pkg won ton wrappers
1/2 cup ground beef
1/2 cup ground pork
1 1/2 cups grated sharp
cheddar cheese
1 1/2 cups Monterey Jack
cheese

1 cup ranch dressing
1 cup finely sliced black olives
1/2 cup finely chopped green
onion
1 1/2 cups finely chopped red
pepper

To make shells take two won ton wrappers and crisscross in muffin pan so that points create a star shape. Be very careful when peeling the wrappers off stack to ensure you are only getting one (they should be very thin). Bake at 305°F for 5 minutes or just a little less depending on oven. Watch very closely that they only get very slightly golden; do not let the tips get too dark.

Brown pork and beef in fry pan and drain excess fat. Add all other ingredients mixing well. Fill shells about 2/3 full, place on cookie sheet and bake at 350°F for about 20 minutes. Heat until cheese is bubbling. Serve warm.

What really matters is what happens in us, not to us.

HOT ROASTED VEGETABLE WRAPS *Sandy Taylor*

1 Tbsp butter, at room
   temperature
1 Tbsp chopped fresh parsley
3 (8 inch) flour tortillas,
   preferably four-cheese
1 lb roasted or grilled
   vegetables, chopped (such
   as peppers, onions, zucchini,
   and mushrooms)

1 Tbsp chopped scallion
1 cup shredded Mexican
   cheese blend
1 1/2 tsp grated Parmesan
   cheese
2/3 cup marinara pasta sauce
   from a jar
1/2 tsp ground cumin

Preheat oven to 400°F. Combine butter and parsley; spread over one side of each tortilla. Place on ungreased baking sheet butter-side down. Combine vegetables and scallion. Place vegetables and shredded cheese in log shape down centers of tortilla; roll up. Sprinkle with Parmesan. Bake until heated through and crisp, 8 to 10 minutes. Cut each wrap into 4 pieces. Combine marinara sauce with cumin; serve with wraps. Makes 12 pieces.

TORTILLA WRAPS *Wendy Ternowesky*

4 (10 inch) flour tortillas
1 large pkg cream cheese
1 cup finely chopped cooked
   chicken
1 cup Monterey Jack cheese,
   grated
1/3 cup finely chopped red
   pepper

2 Tbsp jalapeno pepper, finely
   chopped
1/4 cup fresh coriander,
   chopped
2 tsp ground cumin
Optional Dips:
Salsa and/or sour cream

Mix all of the above, except the tortillas, in a large bowl; divide into 4. Spread each tortilla with 1/4 of the mixture. Roll up tightly. Wrap in plastic. Refrigerate for at least 2 hours or up to 24 hours, or freeze (if freezing, pre-cut into 1/2 inch pieces). Cut into 1/2 inch pieces. Bake on cookie sheet at 350°F for 12 to 15 minutes. Serve hot, alone, or with dips of salsa and/or sour cream.

Trying times are times for trying.

SPICED CASHEWS OR PECANS   *Trish Markwick*

2 cups nuts, halved
1 1/2 Tbsp melted butter
1 tsp salt

2 tsp soya sauce
1/8 tsp Tabasco sauce

Preheat oven to 300°F. Place nuts in a baking pan. Melt butter and pour over nuts. Mix remaining ingredients and pour over nuts. Bake for 15 to 20 minutes. Stir and toss nuts during cooking time.

SPICED NUTS

1 large egg white
1/4 cup sugar
1 tsp salt
1/2 tsp chili powder
1/4 tsp ground allspice

1/2 tsp ground cumin
1 3/4 tsp cayenne pepper
2 1/2 cups pecan halves or
   assorted nuts, such as
   cashews, walnuts or almonds

Preheat oven to 300°F. Beat egg white until soft and foamy. Combine all remaining ingredients except pecans; whisk into egg white. Stir in pecans, or other nuts, until well coated; spread mixture in single layer onto an ungreased baking pan. Bake nuts for 15 minutes, then remove from the oven. Using a metal spatula, toss, stir and separate nuts. Reduce oven to 250°F, and return nuts to bake until medium brown, about 10 minutes. Remove from oven; toss, and stir again. Place baking pan on wire rack to cool (they will crisp as they cool). Break up any that stick together. Store in airtight container, at room temperature for up to 2 weeks.

CASHEW NUT BRITTLE   *Sharon Roberts*

1 1/2 cups unsalted cashews
1 cup white sugar
1/2 cup white corn syrup
1/2 tsp salt

1 tsp butter
1 tsp vanilla
1 tsp baking soda

Line a baking sheet with foil. Spread some butter on the foil surface and set aside. In 6 cup microwave safe bowl, combine sugar, corn syrup and salt. Cook uncovered for 3 minutes on high in microwave. Stir well, cook another 3 minutes. Stir in butter, vanilla and nuts. Cook for 2 to 3 minutes. Add baking soda and stir until foamy, quickly pour onto foil and spread. Let cool and break into bite-sized pieces.

CINNAMON COFFEE FLOAT

Sandy Taylor

1/2 cup vanilla ice cream
1/8 tsp ground cinnamon

3/4 cup hot brewed coffee
Cinnamon stick

Place ice cream and ground cinnamon in a mug. Pour hot coffee over top. Add cinnamon stick.

HOT BUTTERED RUM

Sandy Taylor

2 cups vanilla ice cream
1 cup butter, softened
1 1/4 cups packed brown sugar
2 cups powdered sugar
1 tsp ground cinnamon

1/2 tsp ground cloves
1 1/4 cups or more dark rum
Boiling water
Cinnamon sticks

Let ice cream soften slightly. In large bowl, cream butter and brown sugar together. Beat in powdered sugar, nutmeg, cinnamon, and cloves. Stir in ice cream until smooth. Place butter in plastic container and freeze until ready to use. To serve spoon 3 tablespoons batter into mug. Add 1 tablespoon rum or more to taste. Fill mug with boiling water. Add cinnamon stick to mug.

SPARKLING CRANBERRY PUNCH

Maureen Cockburn

1 qt cranberry juice, chilled
1 can frozen pink lemonade

2 qt gingerale or 2 (750 mL)
 bottles Champagne, chilled

Serves 25.

If you want to know how many friends you have, just buy a cottage on a lake.

WASSAIL

Sandy Taylor

Peel of 1 lemon
3 slices peeled fresh ginger
  root
1 stick cinnamon
1 tsp whole allspice

6 cups (1.5 L) dry red wine or
  cranberry juice
6 cups (1.5 L) apple cider
1/2 cup sugar
2 oranges, unpeeled, cut into 6
  wedges each
36 whole cloves

Place lemon peel, ginger root, cinnamon, and allspice on a small piece of cheesecloth or in a paper coffee filter. Bundle up the corners and tie top with kitchen string, leaving excess string to hang out of pot for easy retrieval. Set sachet aside.

In 6-quart Dutch oven, combine wine, apple cider, and sugar. Add sachet. Bring to boil over high heat, stirring until sugar is dissolved. Cover, reduce heat to medium-low. Simmer for 15 minutes. Remove sachet. Keep wassail warm over low heat. While wassail simmers, stick 3 whole cloves into peel side of each orange wedge. Place one wedge in each serving cup and ladle hot wassail over top. Serve hot.

HOT MULLED WINE

Audrey Karpoff

4 cups sugar
1 Tbsp cinnamon or 6 medium
  cinnamon sticks
1 tsp ground cloves or whole
  cloves

3 medium oranges, thinly sliced
1 medium lemon, thinly sliced
1 gallon (16 cups) dry red wine

About 30 minutes before serving, in an 8-quart saucepot, over high heat, heat first 5 ingredients and 2 cups water to boiling. Boil for 5 minutes, stirring occasionally. Reduce heat to medium, pour in wine and heat until piping hot but not boiling. Stir occasionally. Serve wine hot. Makes about 18 cups or thirty-six 1/2 cup servings.

Salads & Dressings
Soups & Sauces

FOOD QUANTITIES TO SERVE 50 PEOPLE

Item	Serving Portion	Amount for 50 People*
Beverages		
Cocoa, mixed	¾ cup	40 cups
unsweetened powder		½ lb.
Coffee	¾ cup	1½ lb.
Punch	½ cup	25 cups
Tea	¾ cup	½ lb.
Bread and Crackers		
Bread	1 slice	4 loaves
Rolls	1 roll	5 doz.
Crackers (soda)	2 crackers	1½-2 lb.
Cereals		
Macaroni, noodles, spaghetti	½ cup	3-4 lb.
Rice	½ cup	4½-5 lb.
Dairy Products		
Butter, for table	1 tbsp.	1-1½ lb.
for vegetables	½ tsp.	¾ lb.
Cheddar cheese	1-1½ oz.	3-5 lb.
Cream, coffee	2 tbsp.	7 cups
whipping		3 cups
Ice cream	½ cup	25 cups
Milk	1 cup	50 cups
Desserts		
Cakes, angel food		3-4 cakes
pound or loaf		4 loaves
8x8-inch square		3-4 cakes
Cookies or slices	3 pieces	150 pieces
Pies	⅛ pie	6 pies
Fish		
Fillets	3 oz.	14-16 lb.
Whole	3 oz.	40 lb.
Fruits		
Apples	1	15 lb.
Bananas	1	16 lb.
Peaches	1	12-15 lb.
Raspberries or strawberries	½ cup	14 lb.
Juice, fruit or vegetable	½ cup	25 cups

Item	Serving Portion	Amount for 50 People*
Meat		
Beef, ground	3 oz.	13-15 lb.
boneless round, rump	3 oz.	16-18 lb.
Lamb, boneless leg	3 oz.	15 lb.
Pork, boneless loin	3 oz.	18-20 lb.
boneless ham	3 oz.	15 lb.
Salami	3 oz.	10 lb.
Sliced luncheon meat	1 oz.	3½ lb.
Weiners	2 weiners	10 lb.
Poultry		
Chicken, fryers	¼ fryer	13 fryers
Turkey	3 oz.	36 lb.
Pickles		
Dill or sweet		10 cups
Relish		8 cups
Salads		
Green	¾ cup	32-40 cups
Potato, chicken or fruit	½ cup	28-32 cups
Salad dressings		
Mayonnaise	1 tbsp.	4 cups
French	2 tsp.	3-4 cups
Sandwiches		
Main meal	1½	70-80
Afternoon	1	50
Vegetables		
Asparagus	½ cup	18-20 lb.
Beans, green or wax	½ cup	10-12 lb.
Broccoli	½ cup	16-20 lb.
Cabbage	1 wedge	12-14 lb.
Cauliflower	½ cup	16-18 lb.
Celery, sticks	4 sticks	4-5 lb.
Corn on the cob	1 ear	5 doz.
Lettuce, for tossed salad	1 cup	8 doz.
for salad plate		8-10 heads
Potatoes, baked	1 potato	17-25 lb.
mashed	½ cup	15 lb.
Tomatoes, sliced	3 slices	15 lb.
Frozen vegetables		10 lb.

*Based on one serving portion per person. For second helpings or larger serving portions, prepare additional food accordingly.

SALADS & DRESSINGS

CAESAR SALAD DRESSING
(With Bite, But No Anchovies)
Lorraine Giordano

1/2 to 3/4 cup olive oil
1 Tbsp Worcestershire sauce
Several drops Tabasco sauce
1/4 tsp dry mustard
2 to 3 large cloves garlic,
   crushed

3 Tbsp red wine vinegar
1 Tbsp lemon juice
3 to 4 Tbsp Parmesan cheese
3/4 tsp seasoning salt
1/4 tsp black pepper
1 large egg

Blend above ingredients at high speed until thick, approximately 1 1/2 to 2 minutes. This may be stored in your fridge for up to a week. Pour on cleaned, torn romaine lettuce, and toss. Add croutons, as desired. Top with more Parmesan cheese or shred some Asiago cheese for a great flavor.

GREEK SALAD
Wendy Ternowesky

1/2 cup Crisco oil
1/4 cup red wine vinegar
2 Tbsp dried parsley flakes
1/2 tsp salt
1/2 tsp pepper
1/2 tsp oregano
1/4 tsp garlic powder
1/2 head romaine lettuce, torn
   into bite-sized pieces
1/2 head lettuce, torn into
   bite-sized pieces

2 tomatoes, cut into bite-sized
   pieces
1 English cucumber, cut into
   bite-sized chunks
1 green pepper, seeded, cut
   into strips
1 small red onion, sliced and
   broken into rings (or 1/4 cup
   green onions, sliced)
1/4 cup ripe olives, sliced
3/4 cup feta cheese, crumbled

Mix first 7 dressing ingredients in morning to blend flavours. combine all salad ingredients, except the feta in a large bowl. Pour salad dressing over salad and toss. Sprinkle feta over salad.

We always weaken what we exaggerate.

ROMAINE WITH ORANGES AND PECANS   *Jackie Pawson*

2 head romaine lettuce, wash
  and tear into bite-sized
  pieces
1 cup pecan halves, toasted
2 oranges, peeled and sliced or
  2 avocados, sliced or 1 cup
  dried cranberries

1/4 cup vinegar
1/2 cup vegetable oil
1/4 cup sugar
1 tsp salt
1/2 small red onion, chopped
1 tsp dry mustard
2 Tbsp water

Place lettuce, pecans and oranges in salad bowl. Combine rest of the ingredients in blender to make dressing. Blend until well mixed. Make ahead and refrigerate until ready to toss salad.

ROMAINE ORANGE SALAD   *Patricia McKinnon*

1 head romaine, chopped
4 green onions, chopped
4 stalks celery, chopped
  (optional)
1 pkg slivered almonds,
  toasted
1 can mandarin oranges,
  drained

1 cup dry chow mein noodles
  (optional)
1/4 cup oil
1 1/2 Tbsp vinegar
1 1/2 Tbsp sugar
1 tsp Tabasco sauce
Salt and pepper, to taste

Place first 6 ingredients in a bowl. Mix oil, vinegar, sugar, Tabasco and salt and pepper and pour over salad.

MIXED GREENS & BEET SALAD   *Gretchen Hopkins*

10 oz can mandarin oranges,
  undrained
1/2 cup raspberry vinaigrette
  dressing
4 cups mixed salad greens

14 oz can beets, drained and
  cut into slivers
1/2 cup almonds, chopped
1/2 small red onion, thinly
  sliced

Drain mandarin oranges, reserving 2 tablespoons juice; add to dressing. Mix greens, mandarin oranges, beets, almonds and red onion in large bowl. Mix lightly with dressing.

CARAWAY SALAD

Cathy Guarasci

10 oz spinach
1 head lettuce
1 Tbsp diced onion
1 Tbsp diced green pepper
1 large orange, peeled and
    chopped or 2 tins mandarin
    oranges

3/4 cup light mayonnaise
2 Tbsp honey
1 Tbsp lemon juice
1 Tbsp caraway seeds

Toss salad, but do not mix in dressing until ready to serve. When ready to serve mix mayonnaise, honey, lemon juice and caraway seeds and pour over salad.

SPINACH SALAD

Ann Bishop

8 cups spinach leaves, torn into
    pieces if large
1 avocado, sliced
1/2 cup sliced red onion
1/2 cup dried cranberries

Dressing:
1/4 cup cranberry juice
    concentrate
1/4 cup white wine vinegar
1 1/2 tsp Dijon style mustard
1/4 tsp pepper
1/2 cup vegetable oil

In large bowl, put spinach, avocado, onion and cranberries. Mix dressing ingredients and pour over salad.

GRAPE SPINACH SALAD

Marge Gale

4 cups spinach, stems
    removed, lightly packed
1 cup sliced fresh strawberries
1/2 cup seedless green grapes,
    halved
1/2 cup seedless red grapes,
    halved

1/4 cup sunflower seeds,
    toasted
2 Tbsp peanut oil
2 Tbsp balsamic vinegar
1 Tbsp maple (or maple
    flavoured) syrup
1 Tbsp poppy seeds
1/4 tsp salt

Arrange spinach on 4 individual salad plates. Top with strawberries, green and red grapes and sunflower seeds. Combine peanut oil, vinegar, syrup, poppy seeds and salt, in a jar with a tight fitting lid. Shake well. Drizzle over spinach mixture. Serves 4.

SPINACH AND BLUEBERRY SALAD   *Marge Gale*

6 oz (170 g) bag of Spinach, stems removed
1 cup fresh blueberries
1/2 cup pecans, toasted and coarsely chopped
6 slices bacon, cooked crisp and crumbled

1/4 cup olive oil
3 Tbsp finely grated Parmesan cheese
2 Tbsp white wine vinegar
1 tsp granulated sugar
1/4 tsp coarsely ground pepper

Put first 4 ingredients into large bowl. Toss. To make dressing process all 5 ingredients in a blender. Process until smooth. Drizzle over spinach mixture. Toss. Makes about 10 cups.

SHRIMP SPINACH SALAD   *Patricia McKinnon*

1/2 cup cooked shrimp
2 bunches baby spinach
1 cup chopped mushrooms
1 red apple, chopped
1/4 cup red onion, chopped
1/4 cup shredded carrot
1/4 cup raisins

4 oz can mandarin oranges, drained
1/4 cup oil
1 1/2 Tbsp vinegar
1 1/2 Tbsp sugar
1 tsp Tabasco sauce
Salt and pepper, to taste

Place first 8 ingredients in a bowl. Make dressing by mixing oil, vinegar, sugar, Tabasco and salt and pepper and pour over salad.

BROCCOLI SALAD   *Gretchen Hopkins*

10 bacon slices, finely diced
1 large head broccoli cut into florets, stems peeled and chopped
1 small red onion, halved lengthwise and thinly sliced
1 cup golden raisins

Dressing:
1 cup mayonnaise (not salad dressing)
1/4 cup granulated sugar
2 Tbsp white vinegar
2 tsp chopped dried chives
2/3 cup salted sunflower seeds, toasted

Cook bacon in large frying pan until almost crisp. Remove to paper towel to drain. Add to broccoli, onion and raisins. Toss. Combine dressing ingredients and pour over salad. Toss to combine.

BROCCOLI SALAD

Dorothy Cunningham

2 bunches broccoli, cut into
  florets
Cauliflower (optional), cut into
  florets
1 medium red onion, diced
1 cup raisins (optional)

1 cup shredded sharp cheddar
  cheese
8 slices crisp bacon, crumbled
1 cup mayonnaise (not Miracle
  Whip)
1/3 cup sugar
2 Tbsp vinegar

Mix salad ingredients in a salad bowl. Mix mayonnaise, sugar and vinegar to make dressing. Pour over salad.

FESTIVE BROCCOLI SALAD

Patricia McKinnon

2 cups mayonnaise
1/2 cup red wine vinegar
1/2 cup sugar
3/4 tsp freshly ground pepper
1/2 tsp salt
2 lb broccoli, trimmed
2 cups shredded cheddar
  cheese

1 cup dried cranberries or
  raisins
1 cup slivered dried apricots
1 cup finely chopped red onion
1 can mandarin oranges,
  drained
4 slices bacon, cooked and
  crumbled

Dressing: Whisk together mayonnaise, vinegar, sugar, pepper and salt, until blended. Set aside.

Cut florets from broccoli. Cut stalks into 1 inch pieces. Place florets in a food processor. Process, using an on/off motion until finely chopped. Repeat procedure with stalk pieces. There should be about 8 cups of chopped florets and stalks. Combine broccoli and remaining ingredients (cheese through bacon) in a bowl. Add dressing and toss to combine. Cover and refrigerate for at least 2 hours or up to 24 hours. Serves 12.

BROCCOLI FETA SALAD

Cathy Guarasci

3 cups raw broccoli
1/2 cup feta cheese, chopped
1/2 cup sunflower seeds
1/2 cup red onion, chopped

1 Tbsp lemon juice
1/2 cup yogurt or sour cream
  (light)
1/3 cup mayonnaise (light)

Toss together and serve.

CORONATION CHICKEN SALAD
Dorinda Torrance

8 boneless skinless chicken
  breasts, halved
1/4 cup oil
1 onion, thinly sliced
1/2 cup mango chutney

2 Tbsp (rounded) tomato paste
1 Tbsp curry powder
1 tsp salt
1 cup mayonnaise
1 Tbsp lemon juice

Place chicken breasts in medium skillet with water to cover. Bring to boil, reduce heat and simmer until chicken is opaque and juices run clear when pricked with fork. Remove chicken from skillet and let cool.

Heat oil in skillet, over medium-low heat. Add onion and cook until wilted, about 5 minutes. Add chutney, tomato paste, curry powder and salt and cook, stirring occasionally, 7 minutes. Remove from heat and let cool. Puree chutney mixture in food processor until smooth. Add mayonnaise and lemon juice and process until incorporated. Add to chicken and toss to coat well. Garnish with cilantro and ginger sticks if desired.

OVERNIGHT COLESLAW
Gretchen Hopkins

1 medium head cabbage,
  shredded
1 chopped green pepper
1 chopped medium red onion
2 shredded carrots
1 cup sugar

Dressing:
2 tsp sugar
1 tsp dry mustard
1 1/2 tsp celery seed
1 tsp salt
1 cup vinegar
1/2 cup vegetable oil

Combine coleslaw ingredients and set aside.

Dressing: Combine ingredients and bring to a boil. Pour over vegetables, stir to cover evenly. Cover and refrigerate overnight.

TOMATO & BOCCONCINI SALAD
Maureen Cockburn

3 large ripe tomatoes
6 oz bocconcini or mozzarella
  cheese, sliced

1 Tbsp extra-virgin olive oil
Freshly ground black pepper
8 to 10 fresh basil leaves

Slice tomatoes into 1/4 inch slices. On large serving platter, arrange tomatoes, overlapping slices slightly. Arrange slices of cheese on top of tomatoes. Drizzle with olive oil, sprinkle generously with black pepper. Stack basil leaves, one on top of the other. With sharp knife slice leaves into thin strips; scatter evenly over tomatoes and cheese. Let stand for 20 to 30 minutes at room temperature before serving.

SALMON, DILL AND ASPARAGUS PASTA SALAD

Kay MacCormack

2 cups penne pasta shells, cooked
1/2 lb fresh asparagus (raw)
1/2 cup green onion
1/2 cup chopped celery
2 cans salmon (or use fresh cooked salmon)

Fresh picked snow peas (optional)
1/4 cup plain yogurt
2 Tbsp light mayonnaise
1 clove garlic, minced
2 Tbsp chopped light dill
1 Tbsp lemon juice
Salt and pepper

Mix vegetables together. In a separate bowl, mix mayonnaise, garlic, dill, lemon juice and salt and pepper. Pour over vegetables and toss.

CUCUMBER NOODLE SALAD

Pat Johnston

7 oz rice noodles
1 Tbsp sesame oil
1/4 cup low-sodium soy sauce
2 Tbsp fresh grated ginger
1 Tbsp chili paste (add more for hotter)
1 Tbsp lemon juice
2 Tbsp rice wine vinegar

1 tsp brown sugar
1 tsp salt
1 seedless cucumber, diced
3 green onions, chopped
1/2 red pepper, diced
1/2 cup salted raw peanuts, roasted in oven 10 minutes

Cook noodles 3 minutes in boiling water, drain, rinse in cold water, drain and toss with sesame oil. Combine soy sauce, ginger, chili paste, vinegar, sugar, lemon juice and salt in a small bowl and toss with noodles. Add cucumber, onion and red peppers 1/2 hour before serving. Add peanuts when serving.

ISLAND FRESH CUCUMBER SALAD

Patricia McKinnon

1/2 lb cooked salad shrimp
1 medium cucumber, peeled, seeded, and thinly sliced
1 tomato, cut into wedges
1/2 white onion, thinly sliced and separated into rings

1/2 cup sweetened rice vinegar
1 Tbsp soy sauce
1 tsp sugar
1/2 tsp sesame oil
1/4 tsp black pepper

Combine vegetables in a large bowl. Make dressing in a small bowl. Pour over vegetables. Add shrimp and toss.

WARM BEET SALAD
WITH BALSAMIC VINEGAR
Audrey Karpoff

8 fresh medium-sized beets,
  peeled and quartered
4 Tbsp olive oil
3 Tbsp balsamic vinegar
2 Tbsp chopped parsley

2 pinches nutmeg
Salt and pepper, to taste
Zest and juice of 1 orange
1/4 cup Italian parsley, coarsely
  chopped

Combine all ingredients, except the parsley, in a large oven proof dish. Make sure the beets are well coated with liquid. Cover and bake at 350°F for 45 to 50 minutes, stirring from time to time, until beets are tender. Garnish with Italian parsley and serve. Can be made ahead of time and stored in the refrigerator for up to 24 hours. Reheat before serving.

CARROT COPPER PENNY SALAD
Rita Bell

8 large carrots
1 onion, sliced and separated
  into rings
1 green pepper, chopped
10 oz can tomato soup
1/2 cup vegetable oil
1/2 cup sugar

3/4 cup vinegar
1 tsp prepared mustard
1 Tbsp Worcestershire sauce
1/2 tsp salt
1 tsp pepper
1 tsp dill seed

Peel, slice and cook carrots until tender. Drain. Cool. Add onion and pepper to carrots. Combine the remaining ingredients. Pour over vegetables and refrigerate for 12 hours before serving.

POTATO SALAD
Kay MacCormack

1 cup Hellmann's light
  mayonnaise or low fat
  mayonnaise
2 Tbsp Dijon mustard
2 Tbsp chopped dill or parsley
2 Tbsp vinegar

1/2 tsp salt
1/4 tsp pepper
2 lb small red potatoes, cooked
  and quartered
1 cup chopped celery
1/2 cup chopped green onion

Combine first six ingredients, stir in potatoes, celery and onion. Cover and chill. Makes 6 cups.

GINGER SALAD DRESSING

Marilyn Kelm

5 Tbsp vegetable oil
2 Tbsp olive oil
2 Tbsp rice vinegar
2 Tbsp lemon juice

2 tsp Dijon mustard
1 tsp ground ginger
Salt and pepper

Combine all ingredients in a screw-top jar and shake to blend.

SOUPS & SAUCES

GAZPACHO ANDALUSIA

Olga Langevin

5 medium, fresh ripe tomatoes, chopped
1 medium Bermuda onion, chopped
2 garlic cloves, peeled and chopped
2 medium cucumbers, peeled and chopped
1 small green pepper, seeded and chopped

1 pimiento, chopped
3 cups cold water
3 cups fresh white bread, crusts removed (Italian or French bread best)
1/4 cup olive oil
3 Tbsp wine vinegar
1 Tbsp chopped fresh parsley
1 Tbsp salt
Pepper, to taste

Combine ingredients in large bowl. Put a few cupfuls at a time in blender and puree. Pour into large container and chill thoroughly. Serve in tureen or large bowl surrounded by small bowls holding various garnishes. Garnish with diced tomatoes, chopped hard-boiled eggs, cucumber, green pepper, and Bermuda onion. Serves 6 to 8.

WATERMELON GAZPACHO

Dorothy Cunningham

4 lb seedless watermelon, without rind (half a large)
1 yellow pepper
1 green pepper
6 oz zucchini
1 clove garlic, put through a press

1/4 tsp salt
3 Tbsp lime juice
Pinch red pepper or few drops hot sauce
2 Tbsp minced red onion
1/4 cup packed mint leaves, chopped

Process the watermelon until liquid. Pour into a large bowl. Process the vegetables coarsely and add to the bowl. Add garlic, salt, lime juice and red pepper. Add mint and red onion for garnish. Chill well before serving. One half cup of vodka adds a little zip. Wonderful summer soup.

LOBSTER BISQUE (Misnomer) — *Gretchen Hopkins*

10 oz can cream of asparagus
   soup
10 oz can cream of mushroom
   soup
6 oz can crab meat, drained

1/4 cup sherry
10 oz can cream
10 oz can milk
A few drops red food colouring

Mix together all ingredients and heat through. Do not boil.

WEST COAST CLAM CHOWDER
VIA MANHATTAN — *Dolly Des Rochers*

8 strips bacon, cubed
2 onions, cut into small cubes
3 cups water
4 stalks celery, cut into small
   cubes
4 medium potatoes, cut into
   cubes

2 small carrots, grated
2 tsp salt
2 cans (28 oz) stewed tomatoes
1 tsp sugar
Pepper, to taste
2 tins clam juice

In saucepan add bacon, onions, water, stir and bring to boil. Add celery, potatoes, carrots and salt. Turn down heat to medium. Add stewed tomatoes, sugar and pepper and add clam juice. Turn stove down to low to simmer and let the flavors release.

EASY GOURMET SOUP — *Dorothy Cunningham*

1 pkg Knorr creamy potato
   soup mix

1 pkg Knorr creamy leek soup
   mix
3 to 4 oz Stilton cheese

Prepare the soup mixes as instructed, then mix together. Add the cheese, cut into small pieces, and stir until melted and well mixed. Garnish with chopped chives.

May you live all the days of your life.

24 SOUPS & SAUCES

LENTIL SOUP

Marilyn Kelm

3 Tbsp margarine or butter
1 medium onion, diced
2 cloves garlic, minced
1 large carrot, finely chopped
3/4 cup red or green lentils
1/4 cup brown rice

3 cups chicken broth
2 cups water
2 tsp salt
Freshly ground pepper, to taste
3 Tbsp lemon juice
1 to 2 bay leaves

Heat margarine in large saucepan or small stock pot. Add and sauté onion and garlic, until onion is transparent. Add carrot and cook until carrot is soft. Add lentils and brown rice and stir until brown, about 2 minutes. Add chicken broth, water, salt, pepper, lemon juice and bay leaves and bring to a boil. Reduce heat, cover and simmer until all ingredients are soft, about 45 minutes. Cool slightly; remove bay leaves, process in food processor until coarsely puréed. Return to pot and reheat over low heat. Serve garnished with thin slice of lemon and/or thin slice of dry toast.

GREAT WINTER SOUP

Lois Wilson

2 cans Great Northern Beans,
  rinsed and drained
4 cups vegetable broth
1/2 cup onion, chopped
1 Tbsp chili powder
1 1/2 tsp salt
2 cloves garlic, chopped finely
28 oz can whole tomatoes,
  undrained

4 oz can chopped green
  chilies, undrained
1 cup uncooked small pasta
  shells
1 pkg frozen chopped spinach
8 oz Monterey Jack or cheddar
  cheese

Combine beans and vegetable broth. Add onion, chili powder, salt, and garlic. Heat to boiling. Reduce heat and simmer for about 15 minutes. Stir in remaining ingredients except for cheese. Bring to a boil again and simmer until pasta is done. Remove from heat and add about 4 ounces of cheese directly to soup and sprinkle remaining 4 ounces on top of each bowl, dividing evenly.

If we pause to think, we will have cause to thank.

SUCCOTASH SOUP
Ann Bishop

1 Tbsp vegetable oil
1 cup chopped peeled squash
1 onion, chopped
2 cloves garlic, minced
1 carrot, chopped
1 celery stalk, chopped

1/2 tsp dried thyme
1/2 tsp pepper
4 cups chicken stock
28 oz can diced tomatoes
1 cup frozen corn
1 cup frozen lima beans

In a saucepan, heat oil, cook squash, onion, garlic, carrot, celery, thyme and pepper about 10 minutes, until soft. Add stock, tomatoes, corn and beans and bring mixture to a boil. Cover and simmer until hot.

CARROT CREAM SOUP
Alyson Clifton

1 1/2 lb carrots, sliced or
    spinach, chopped
3/4 cup onion, chopped
2 Tbsp butter
1/2 cup chicken stock

1 cup heavy cream
1/2 tsp curry or 1/4 tsp mace
    for spinach
Salt and pepper, to taste
Herbs to garnish, chopped

Boil carrots until very tender, 9 to 11 minutes. While carrots cook, sauté onions in butter, in a large saucepan, cooking until translucent. Drain carrots; reserve 1 cup of cooking liquid.

In food processor, puree carrots and onions with 1/2 cup of reserved liquid until smooth. In same saucepan, combine pureed carrots, 1/2 cup chicken stock, remaining reserved cooking liquid, cream and curry powder. Season with salt and pepper. Mix well, bring to simmer over medium heat. Serve garnished with chopped herbs. Makes 4 servings.

EASY CARROT SOUP
Barb Bayles

1 lb carrots, chopped
1/2 tsp thyme
1 small onion, chopped
1 clove garlic, minced

8 oz can chicken or vegetable
    broth
3 oz cream cheese
1 tsp curry powder
1 cup milk

Put the first 6 ingredients in a pot and simmer until the onion and carrots are tender. Extra broth or water may be needed if the liquid has reduced too much. Transfer to blender and blend until smooth. Add cream cheese and milk and blend again. Return soup to pot and reheat.

RED PEPPER SOUP
Dorothy Cunningham

2 Tbsp olive oil
1 small red onion, chopped
3 cloves garlic, slivered
1 1/2 cups sliced carrots
4 large sweet red peppers, cut
6 plum tomatoes, chopped
1 red apple, chopped
1 Tbsp paprika

1 tsp each salt, dried thyme,
  marjoram
1 Tbsp brown sugar
Pinch cayenne pepper
1/4 tsp ground allspice
Black pepper
2 Tbsp sherry or cider vinegar
4 cups water

Heat oil and cook onion, garlic and carrots, stirring for 3 to 4 minutes. Add red peppers, tomatoes, and apple and cook, stirring occasionally for about 15 minutes. Add paprika, salt, sugar, thyme, marjoram, allspice, cayenne and black pepper to taste. Cook 3 minutes. Add vinegar and bring to a boil and boil 2 minutes. Add 4 cups water, return to a boil, stirring. Reduce heat to low and cook, covered, for 1 hour. Stir occasionally. Cool to warm, and puree. Peel tomatoes for a smoother soup. Refrigerate up to 2 days. Freezes well. Also good warm.

SPINACH AND FENNEL SOUP
Dorothy Cunningham

1/4 cup butter
1 fennel bulb (about 1/2 lb
  peeled and cut julienne,
  about 2 cups) (may use anise
  seed to taste, it is quicker)
1 medium onion, chopped
4 cups chicken stock
1/2 bunch parsley, stems
  removed and tied together

1 lb spinach, stemmed and
  coarsely chopped
1/2 tsp dried tarragon,
  crumbled
1 cup half and half (or Lactaid)
Salt and pepper, to taste
Minced parsley and sour cream
  for garnish

Melt butter over low heat, in heavy saucepan. Add fennel and onion. Cover and cook, about 10 minutes, until onion is soft. Add chicken stock and parsley stems. Increase heat to high and bring to a boil. Reduce heat to medium, cover and simmer for 10 to 15 minutes. Add spinach and cook for 5 minutes. Discard parsley stems. Allow to cool a bit, then in small batches, blend until smooth. Return to saucepan, place over medium heat and bring to a simmer. Add tarragon, simmer for 1 minute. Cover and set aside for 1 minute and then blend in half and half. Season with salt and pepper. Reheat if necessary, but do not boil. Garnish with minced parsley and sour cream.

ZUCCHINI AND APPLE SOUP

Olga Langevin

1 large apple (Rome Beauty,
  Northern Spy, Winesap)
2 Tbsp butter
1 Tbsp olive oil
2 medium zucchini, chopped
1 large onion, sliced
1/2 cup cider or sherry
1/2 tsp ground nutmeg

1/2 tsp freshly ground black
  pepper
4 cups chicken or vegetable
  stock
1/2 cup light cream
1/2 cup chopped fresh parsley
Ground nutmeg (optional)

Peel, core and dice the apple. Heat the butter and oil in a large skillet. Add the apple, zucchini, and onion; sauté over medium heat (350°F) for 5 to 10 minutes, until soft. Add cider, nutmeg, and pepper. Cover the pan and simmer for 15 minutes longer. Add the stock, cover the pan, and simmer for 5 minutes. Puree the vegetables in a blender or food processor (or force through a sieve). Return vegetables to the skillet, add the cream, and bring to a fast boil. Pour into serving bowls and sprinkle with the parsley. Dust with additional pepper, and a little ground nutmeg.

BUTTERNUT SQUASH SOUP

Dorothy Cunningham

1 large butternut squash,
  peeled, seeded and cubed
6 cups chicken broth
2 cups baking potatoes, peeled
  and cubed
1 cup Vidalia (or sweet) onion,
  chopped
1 fresh pear, peeled, cored and
  chopped

1 Tbsp garlic, chopped
1 tsp fresh ginger, minced
3/4 cup whipping cream (homo
  milk or Lactaid)
1/4 cup fresh orange juice
1 Tbsp fresh lemon juice
1 tsp salt
1 tsp hot chili sauce

Combine the first 7 ingredients in a large pot, bring to a boil, cover, reduce heat and simmer for 40 minutes, or until tender. Cool slightly, and process in small batches until smooth. Return puree to pot, add cream and remaining ingredients. Heat until thoroughly warm (do not boil). Taste, and adjust seasonings. Makes 3 quarts. Good hot or cold. Freezes well.

Luck is always against the person who depends upon it.

CURRIED SWEET POTATO SOUP

Gail Robertson

2 Tbsp olive oil
1 medium onion, chopped
1 medium sweet red pepper,
  seeded and chopped
3 to 4 garlic cloves, chopped
2 Tbsp fresh ginger, chopped
  or grated
1 Tbsp curry powder

3 medium sweet potatoes,
  peeled and chopped
5 cups chicken or vegetable
  stock
1/4 cup whipping cream
Salt and pepper, to taste
Green onions, chopped, for
  garnish

Heat oil in a pot over medium heat, then add onions and red pepper. Cook until vegetables are tender, about 5 minutes. Add garlic, ginger and curry powder and cook 1 to 2 minutes more. Add sweet potatoes and stock and gently simmer until potatoes are tender. Cool. Puree mixture in a blender or food processor in small batches. Return to pot, reheat, add cream and gently simmer and season to taste with salt and pepper. Garnish with green onions and, if desired, some finely chopped red pepper and a few thin streams of cream poured over top. Soup can be made a day or two in advance and reheated.

CURRIED CELERY SOUP

Lorraine Giordano

4 cups chopped celery
3/4 cup chopped onions
1 1/2 cups cubed potato
3 Tbsp butter
3 cups chicken stock

1 1/2 tsp curry powder
2 cups milk (2% or
  homogenized)
1 can shrimp

Melt butter over medium heat in a large soup pot. Add veggies. Gently cook onion, potato, and celery until translucent. Add chicken stock, bring to a boil, then reduce heat and simmer for 60 to 90 minutes, stirring occasionally. Stir in curry, and then turn heat off. Let mixture cool, then puree in blender or food processor. Reheat on medium heat; add milk, stirring constantly. Do not let soup boil. Serve immediately with topping of fresh celery leaves, paprika or drained shrimp (optional). You can make the vegetable mixture and puree it, then freeze it. Just add milk after it is thawed, heated and ready to eat.

Failure is a temporary detour, not a dead end street.

HAMBURGER SOUP
Sandy Taylor

1 lb lean ground beef
1 stalk celery, chopped
1 large carrot, peeled and
  sliced
1 onion, chopped
1 clove garlic, minced
1 tsp vegetable oil
28 oz can diced tomatoes,
  including juice
14 oz can red kidney beans,
  drained and rinsed

10 oz can condensed tomato
  soup, undiluted
1/2 cup sliced mushrooms
2 tsp Worcestershire sauce
Pinch cayenne pepper
Salt and freshly ground black
  pepper, to taste
1 zucchini, chopped
2 Tbsp chopped fresh parsley
Freshly grated Parmesan
  cheese

In a non-stick skillet over medium heat, brown ground beef until no longer pink. Break up ground beef as it cooks. With a slotted spoon, transfer ground beef to Dutch oven. In same non-stick skillet, sauté celery, carrot, onion and garlic for 5 minutes or until softened. Add this to the Dutch oven. Add diced tomatoes, kidney beans, tomato soup, 1 can water, mushrooms, Worcestershire sauce, cayenne pepper, salt, and pepper. Increase heat to medium-high and bring to a boil. Reduce heat to low and simmer, uncovered for 30 minutes, stirring occasionally until thickened and tomatoes have broken down. Add zucchini and parsley and simmer for 15 minutes longer. Serve with Parmesan cheese.

SUMMER PASTA SAUCE - PASTA SALSA!
Paula Watkin

3 lb very ripe tomatoes
1/4 cup extra virgin olive oil
2 cloves garlic, peeled and
  chopped finely
1/4 tsp hot pepper flakes, to
  taste

1 to 2 tsp salt, to taste
1/2 cup chopped Italian parsley
1/4 cup chopped fresh basil
Parmesan as desired

Dice the tomatoes fairly finely, saving all the juice from the cutting board. Put into a glass dish, and stir in the rest of the ingredients. Put in slightly more salt than you think you should. Leave the dish at room temperature for at least 3 hours for the flavours to develop. Serve over hot pasta.

One thing about silence - it can't be repeated.

CHOW-CHOW
Olga Langevin

20 peeled red tomatoes
6 peaches (fresh fruit or 2 tins pears or peaches)
6 pears
6 onions
3 red peppers
3 green peppers

1 large celery stalk (without leaves)
4 cups white sugar
2 Tbsp salt
30 oz white vinegar
1 Tbsp mixed pickling spices

Chop all produce into small pieces. Combine with remaining ingredients in a large heavy pot. Bring to a boil, then lower heat and simmer, uncovered for 2 to 3 hours. Pour into sterilized jars and seal as directed by the manufacturer.

FREEZER TOMATO ZUCCHINI SAUCE
Maureen Cockburn

2 Tbsp oil
2 cups chopped onion
1 clove garlic, minced
2 cups chopped celery
1 green pepper, seeded and chopped
1 red pepper, seeded and chopped
4 medium zucchini, chopped

12 tomatoes, peeled and chopped
1 tsp salt
2 tsp granulated sugar
1/2 tsp freshly ground pepper
2 tsp thyme
1 tsp oregano
1 bay leaf

In a large saucepan heat oil. Sauté onion, garlic, celery, green and red pepper for about 5 minutes or until tender. Add zucchini; cook for 5 minutes. Add remaining ingredients and simmer uncovered for 45 minutes or until sauce is slightly thickened. Ladle sauce into freezer containers. Label, date and freeze. Makes 3 containers.

One of the hardest decisions in life
is when to start middle age.

CHAMPAGNE RAISIN SAUCE

Donna Wisniowski

2 cups champagne or white
  wine, divided
1 cup raisins
4 tsp cornstarch
1 cup granulated sugar

1/4 cup butter
1/2 tsp salt
1/4 tsp ground cloves
1/4 tsp ground cinnamon

In saucepan, bring 1 cup of the champagne and raisins to boil, reduce heat to low and simmer for 5 minutes. Dissolve cornstarch in remaining champagne, add to the saucepan along with sugar, butter, salt, cloves and cinnamon. Cook, stirring until boiling and slightly thickened, 2 to 3 minutes. Pour into sauceboat. Instead of champagne you could use half champagne and half white wine or sherry.

JELLO CRANBERRY RELISH

Gretchen Hopkins

2 1/2 cups orange juice
1 tsp ground cinnamon
1/4 tsp ground cloves
85 g pkg Jello cranberry jelly
  powder

1 cup finely chopped mixed
  dried fruit (apricots, raisins,
  dried cranberries)
1 cup chopped walnuts,
  toasted
1 Tbsp grated orange or lemon
  peel (optional)

Mix juice, cinnamon and cloves in medium saucepan. Bring to boil on medium-high heat. Add to dry gelatin in large bowl; stir at least 2 minutes until gelatin is completely dissolved. Refrigerate about 1 1/2 hours or until thickened (spoon drawn through leaves an impression). Stir in fruit, walnuts and orange peel. Refrigerate for 1 hour or until chilled. Serve with pork.

Vegetables

VEGETABLE COOKING TIMETABLE

	Boil	Steam	Pressure Cook (15 pounds pressure)	Bake (350°F.)
Asparagus, tied in bundles	15-20	30-40	9	
Beans, wax or green	15-25	30-35	2-2.5	
Beets, whole	25-45		15-18	90
Beet greens (tops)	5-15			
Broccoli, stalks	10-15	15-20	1½-3	
Brussels sprouts	10-20	15-20	1-2	
Cabbage, green				
wedges	8-15	10-15	2-3	
shredded	4-8	8-12	½-1½	
Cabbage, red				
shredded	20-25	25-30	3-4	
Carrots, sliced	15-20	20-30	2-3	35-45
Cauliflower,				
whole	15-25	25-30	3-4	
flowerettes	10-15	10-20	1½-3	
Celery, diced	15-20	25-30	2-3	
Corn on the cob	8-10	10-15	½-1½	
Eggplant, sliced	10-20	15-20		30
Onions, small, whole	15-30	25-30	3-4	
Parsnips, quartered	20-30	30-45	10	
Peas	15-20	15-25	1	
Potatoes, whole	30-35	30-45	15	40-60
quartered	20-30	30-35	8	
Squash Hubbard, sliced	35-45	45-50	12-15	60-90
Squash, Summer, sliced	8-15	15-20	1½-3	30
Spinach	4-8	5-12		
Turnips, sliced	15-20	20-25	1½	

(All cooking times are in minutes)

Boiling: Add vegetables to boiling, salted water using as little water as possible. Cover saucepan. Bring water to a boil again and then reduce heat to a gentle boil. Cook until just tender. Drain; season to taste.

Steaming: Place vegetables in steamer basket just over, not touching, rapidly boiling water. Sprinkle with salt, cover, and cook until just tender. Drain; season to taste.

Pressure Cooking: A quick way to cook vegetables; helps retain color, flavor and nutrients. Follow manufacturer's instructions carefully.

Baking: Place prepared vegetables in a greased baking dish with a small amount of water; season, dot with butter, cover and bake. Potatoes and squash are best baked dry in their skin. Baking helps retain color, flavor and nutrients. Vegetables can often be baked in the oven alongside another part of the meal.

Note: Whatever the method of preparation be careful to avoid overcooking. Always cook vegetables until just tender so as to retain color, maximum flavor and nutritional value.

VEGETABLES

ROASTED ASPARAGUS
Sandy Taylor

2 lb (1 kg) fresh asparagus,
   trimmed
2 Tbsp olive oil
1/2 tsp salt
1/2 tsp pepper

1/2 cup olive oil
2 to 3 Tbsp white wine vinegar
1 tsp Dijon mustard
1 tsp minced garlic
1/2 tsp salt

Heat oven to 400°F. Toss asparagus in 2 tablespoons olive oil to coat. Spread in single layer on large baking sheet. Sprinkle evenly with salt and pepper. Roast asparagus for 10 to 12 minutes, just until tender, turning asparagus over once. While asparagus roasts, combine dressing ingredients, olive oil, vinegar, mustard, garlic and salt. Whisk well to combine. Drizzle dressing over hot asparagus.

BROCCOLI AND CAULIFLOWER CASSEROLE
Dolly Des Rochers

Broccoli
Cauliflower
1/2 cup sour cream
1/2 cup sharp cheddar cheese

10 oz tin Campbell's mushroom
   and onion soup
Salt and pepper, to taste
1/2 cup dry bread crumbs
1 Tbsp melted butter

Cook broccoli and cauliflower until barely fork tender. Drain, place in casserole. Mix sour cream, cheddar cheese and soup. Add salt and pepper to taste. Pour mixture over vegetables. Top with mixed melted butter with bread crumbs. Bake for 25 minutes in 375°F oven.

*Only two groups of people fall
for flattery - men and women.*

BROCCOLI CASSEROLE

Vi Sakaki

1 clove garlic, minced
1 large onion, chopped
1/4 cup butter
4 cups broccoli, bite sized
  pieces
10 oz tin cream of mushroom
  soup

7 oz roll sharp cheese snack or
  7 oz Cheez Whiz
10 oz tin sliced mushrooms,
  drained
1/4 cup chopped almonds
1/2 cup buttered dry bread
  crumbs
1/4 cup chopped almonds

Sauté onions, and garlic in butter. Spoon into large greased casserole. Cook broccoli until crunchy. Add to casserole. Add mushrooms and chopped almonds. In a separate bowl, blend mushroom soup and cheese. Fold into casserole. Top with almonds and buttered bread crumbs. Bake in 350°F oven for 45 minutes. Serves 10.

BROCCOLI WITH
RAISINS AND PINE NUTS

Dorinda Torrance

2 large bunches broccoli (about
  3 lb or 1.5 kg)
2 tsp olive oil
2 small onions, chopped

2 garlic cloves, chopped fine
1/2 cup raisins
2 Tbsp pine nuts, toasted
Salt and pepper

Trim broccoli and cut in 2-inch chunks. Bring large pot of water to boil. Add broccoli. Return to boil and cook for 3 to 5 minutes or until just tender. Drain and rinse with cold water to stop cooking and set color and texture. Set aside. In large fry pan, heat oil over medium heat. Add onions and garlic and cook gently until tender (add bit of water if necessary to prevent browning), about 7 minutes. Add raisins and pine nuts and cook for an additional 2 minutes. Add broccoli and toss gently until heated through and coated with onion mixture. Season to taste with salt and pepper.

*Some people are like a callus: they
always show up when the work is finished.*

PECAN BROCCOLI
Sandy Taylor

6 cups broccoli florets
1/2 cup pecans
2 Tbsp butter or margarine
1 Tbsp shallots, chopped
2 cloves garlic, minced

1/2 tsp salt
1/4 tsp pepper
2 Tbsp chopped fresh parsley
1 Tbsp white wine (optional)

Bring large pot of water to a boil. Add broccoli and cook until slightly tender, approximately 2 minutes. Drain. Heat large dry skillet over medium heat. Add pecans; cook for 1 to 2 minutes, stirring, until lightly browned. Remove from skillet; reserve. In same skillet over low heat, melt butter. Add shallots, garlic, salt and pepper. Cook for 1 to 2 minutes, stirring occasionally, until softened. Add parsley and wine; cook 30 seconds. Add broccoli; cook for 1 to 2 minutes, stirring until coated and heated through. Serve sprinkled with pecans.

GREEN BEANS
Lorraine Giordano

1 kg bag frozen green beans
2 Tbsp butter
2 Tbsp flour
1 tsp white sugar
1/4 tsp ground pepper
1 Tbsp grated onion

1 1/2 cups sour cream
1/2 lb white cheese
 (mozzarella, Swiss, or
 Monterey Jack)
2 cups corn flakes
2 Tbsp melted butter

Cook frozen beans, just until water boils, 1 to 2 minutes. Drain. Set aside. Melt butter in saucepan. Stir in flour, sugar, pepper, and onion. Cook for 2 to 3 minutes, and then reduce heat. Add sour cream; stir until smooth. Fold in beans, and then turn into buttered casserole. (Use a shallow large one so more people can enjoy the topping.) Shred cheese and cover mixture in casserole dish. Mix the corn flakes and melted butter; scatter over cheese. Bake in 350°F oven for 20 to 30 minutes or until bubbly and crumbs are turning brown.

They that are good for making excuses
are seldom good for anything else.

FRENCH GREEN BEAN CASSEROLE
Joan Gilbertson

2x10 oz (300 g) pkg frozen
  French green beans
284 mL tin mushroom soup
284 mL tin mushroom stems
  and pieces

3 Tbsp (45 mL) cream or milk
Salt and pepper
1 cup (250 mL) cheddar cheese
Frozen or canned onion rings

Cook beans in juice from mushrooms until most of the juice is gone. Gently mix mushroom soup in with the beans. Add mushroom pieces, cream and seasonings to taste. Put in casserole, sprinkle with grated cheddar cheese and top with onion rings. Cover and bake at 350°F (180°C) for 1 hour. Remove cover for last 15 minutes. Serves 8 to 10.

BAKED GREEN BEANS
Barb Bayles

2 (10 oz) pkg frozen French
  style green beans, cooked
1/2 cup milk

1 can celery soup
1/4 cup margarine or butter
2 slices bread, cubed

Preheat oven to 350°F. Drain beans and pour into greased casserole. Blend soup and milk. Pour over the beans. Bake for 30 minutes. Pour margarine over bread crumbs and sprinkle on top of beans. Bake for 15 minutes more.

GREEN BEANS WITH
GINGERED WALNUTS
Kay MacCormack

1 Tbsp canola oil
1 tsp reduced-sodium soy
  sauce
1/4 tsp ground ginger
1/4 tsp garlic powder

3/4 cup chopped walnut halves
1 lb green beans, rinsed and
  trimmed
1 Tbsp olive oil

Preheat the oven to 250°F. Spread the canola oil in a small baking pan, and place the pan in the oven. When the pan is hot, remove it, and stir in the soy sauce, ginger, and garlic. Add the walnuts, and stir to coat. Bake, stirring occasionally, for 25 minutes, or until the nuts are crisp and brown. Remove the pan from the oven. Cool the nuts on a paper towel. In a bowl, toss the beans with lemon juice and olive oil. Add the walnuts, and toss again. Serve immediately.

CHICK PEA CURRY

Patricia Markwick

2 Tbsp vegetable oil
1 large onion, chopped
1 Tbsp curry powder
2 Tbsp flour
2 cups stock (vegetable or
    chicken bouillon cubes)
1/2 cup raisins

1/4 cup fine coconut
1 apple, chopped
1 tsp tomato ketchup
1 tsp sugar
1 tsp Worcestershire sauce
1 can chick peas, drained and
    rinsed

Sauté onion in oil until tender, about 5 minutes. Stir in curry powder and flour. Add stock stirring constantly. Add all other ingredients except chick peas and simmer for 15 minutes. Stir in chick peas. Add salt if necessary. Make this 1 to 2 days ahead to allow the flavours to blend. Serve hot with rice or cold as a salad.

ORANGE GLAZED CARROTS

Lea Patchell

10 medium carrots, diagonally
    cut
2 Tbsp brown sugar
2 tsp cornstarch

1/2 tsp ground ginger
1/4 tsp salt
1/2 cup orange juice
1/4 cup butter

Cook carrots in boiling salted water until tender crisp. (To cook in microwave, place carrots in bowl or casserole, add a little bit of water and about 1 teaspoon salt. Cook covered, on high for about 5 minutes, or longer if necessary, until tender crisp. Stir a few times during cooking time.) Drain well when cooked.

In a small saucepan, combine sugar, cornstarch, ginger and salt. Add orange juice and cook, stirring constantly until thickened, boiling for 1 minute. Stir in butter and remove from heat. Pour over hot drained carrots, tossing gently to coat evenly. This may be made ahead and chilled. Reheat just before serving time. (Can be done in the microwave.) Serves 8.

*Grandfather had a farm, his son has a
garden and his grandson has a can opener.*

SWISS CORN BAKE

Margaret Roller

29 oz pkg frozen corn
6 oz can evaporated milk
1 egg, beaten
2 Tbsp finely chopped onion
1/2 tsp salt, pepper

3/4 cup shredded Swiss cheese
1/2 cup soft bread crumbs
1 Tbsp melted butter
1/4 cup shredded Swiss cheese

Heat oven to 350°F. Cook corn as directed on package. Combine corn with evaporated milk, egg, onion, salt, pepper and Swiss cheese. Turn into baking dish. Toss bread crumbs, butter and Swiss cheese together. Sprinkle over the top and bake for 25 minutes.

GRILLED FENNEL

Olga Langevin

4 small or 2 large fennel bulbs
1/3 cup olive oil
1/3 cup balsamic vinegar
2 Tbsp honey
2 cloves garlic, minced

2 small shallots, minced
3 Tbsp chopped fresh tarragon
  or basil
Salt and freshly ground pepper,
  to taste

Cut stalks and outside leaves off fennel. Cut each bulb lengthwise into 1/2 inch wide slices through the narrow side. Combine oil, vinegar, honey, garlic, shallots and tarragon in large nonreactive bowl and whisk to mix. Add fennel and toss to coat thoroughly. Cover and let marinate for 2 hours.

Preheat grill to high. When ready to cook, remove fennel slices from marinade, arrange on hot grate and grill, turning with tongs until just tender, 8 to 16 minutes in all, seasoning with salt and pepper. Toss grilled fennel with any remaining marinade and serve warm or at room temperature. Serves 4.

*The closest to perfection some people ever
come is when they fill out a job application.*

GRILLED PORTOBELLO MUSHROOMS
WITH WATERCRESS & PECAN PESTO   *Kathryn Waldie*

6 Portobello mushrooms, about
  3 inches in diameter
6 Tbsp olive oil
Salt and black pepper, to taste
1/2 cup basil leaves
1 cup watercress leaves

2 oz pecans
1/2 cup grated Parmesan
  cheese
1/2 cup extra virgin olive oil
2 cloves garlic, peeled
Salt and pepper, to taste

Rub the mushrooms with the olive oil and sprinkle with salt and pepper. Grill or barbecue on high, skin side down, until you see a bit of juice coming out of the mushrooms. Remove from the grill and let cool. Combine the basil, watercress, pecans, 2 tablespoons of Parmesan cheese, the olive oil and garlic in a food processor and purée until smooth. Season with salt and pepper. Rub the cavity of each mushroom with some of the pesto and sprinkle each one with 1 tablespoon of the remaining Parmesan cheese. Reheat on the grill or in a 350°F oven, cooking until the cheese melts slightly.

ONION PIE   *Maureen Cockburn*

Unbaked pastry shell
3 cups thinly-sliced mild onions
3 Tbsp olive oil
1 Tbsp butter

1/2 tsp dry mustard
1/2 cup cream or milk
6 ripe olives, chopped

Fry onions gently in oil and butter until soft and yellow. Add mustard to cream or milk and combine with the onions. Pour into unbaked pie shell and sprinkle with the olives. Bake for 15 minutes in 450°F oven, then reduce to 350°F and continue baking until filling is set (about 10 minutes longer). Can be made in small tart shells for appetizers.

If you want to see a short summer,
borrow some money due in the fall.

SOUTH AFRICAN PUMPKIN FRITTERS   *Jo-Ann Martin*

750 mL mashed cooked
  pumpkin
2 eggs
5 mL salt
500 mL self rising flour (or 500
  mL flour less 30 mL) flour,
  then add 30 mL baking
  powder)

15 mL baking powder
500 mL cooking oil
500 mL sugar
250 mL water
125 mL milk
30 mL butter
Pinch salt
10 mL cornstarch

Mix pumpkin, eggs and salt together. Sift flour and baking powder together and mix with pumpkin. Heat oil. Spoon spoonfuls into oil. Cook until golden brown on both sides.

To make syrup, heat sugar, water, milk, butter and salt together. Mix cornstarch with 1 tablespoon water and add to mixture to thicken. Cook over low heat, stirring frequently until thick. Dip into syrup and sprinkle with cinnamon.

RED BEAN, SWEET POTATO AND
SUMMER SQUASH GRATIN   *Kathryn Waldie*

3 cups diced sweet potato
2 Tbsp butter or vegetable oil
2 cups diced summer squash
2 cloves garlic, minced
4 to 6 scallions, chopped
1 1/2 cups milk (or coconut
  milk or soy milk)
1 cup cooked or canned red
  kidney beans or cannelloni
  beans, drained

2 Tbsp chopped fresh basil
  leaves (or 2 tsp dried)
1/2 tsp dried thyme
1/2 tsp ground black pepper
1/4 tsp ground cloves
1/4 tsp salt
1 cup shredded Gouda cheese
1/4 cup dried bread crumbs

Place the sweet potatoes in boiling water to cover and boil for about 5 minutes. Drain in a colander and cool slightly. Discard the water. Preheat the oven to 375°F. Melt the butter in a saucepan and add the summer squash, scallions, and garlic and sauté for 5 to 7 minutes. Add the milk, beans, and seasonings and cook over medium heat for about 5 minutes, stirring frequently. Place the potatoes in the bottom of a lightly greased 8 inch square casserole or gratin dish. Pour the vegetable-milk mixture over the potatoes and sprinkle with the Gouda and bread crumbs. Place in the oven and bake for 20 minutes until a crust forms on top. Remove from the oven and serve hot from the baking dish. Yield: 4 servings.

SQUASH GRATIN

Sandy Taylor

2 medium yellow onions,
  chopped
2 Tbsp olive oil
6 cups shredded peeled
  butternut squash
2 Tbsp all purpose flour
2 Tbsp butter, chopped
2 tsp salt

1/2 tsp freshly ground pepper
2 cups shredded Swiss cheese
1 cup whole milk or
  half-and-half
3/4 cup dried bread crumbs
1/2 cup shredded Parmesan
  cheese
3 Tbsp butter, melted

Heat oven to 350°F. In a large skillet, cook onions in oil over medium heat for 20 to 25 minutes, or until onions are a deep golden brown (caramelized), stirring occasionally. While onions cook, grease a 3 quart casserole dish. Spread 2 cups squash in prepared casserole. Top with half the onions, 1 tablespoon flour, 1 tablespoon butter, 1 teaspoon salt, and 1/4 teaspoon pepper. Sprinkle 1 cup cheese over top. Repeat. Top with remaining squash. Pour milk over top.

Combine topping ingredients, bread crumbs, Parmesan cheese and melted butter. Sprinkle evenly over squash. Tent with foil. Bake for 50 to 60 minutes, or until top is golden brown and gratin is bubbly around edges. Remove foil after 30 minutes.

RUM PINEAPPLE SQUASH

Kay MacCormack

4 cups cooked mashed squash
1/2 cup crushed pineapple,
  drained overnight

2 Tbsp maple syrup
2 Tbsp dark rum
1 Tbsp butter

Mix all ingredients in a casserole dish and bake at 350°F for 30 minutes. Top with walnuts or pecans.

*A bore is someone who, when
you ask how they are, tells you.*

MUSTARD RING

Marianne Routley

4 eggs
1 cup water
1/2 cup cider vinegar
3/4 cup sugar
1 Tbsp unflavored gelatin
4 tsp dry mustard
1/4 tsp turmeric
1/2 tsp salt

1 1/2 cups sour cream
1/4 cup finely sliced green
  onions
Optional:
Raw cauliflower
Tender crisp zucchini slices
Vinaigrette or other dressing

Beat eggs in top of double boiler with water and vinegar. Thoroughly combine sugar, gelatin, mustard, turmeric and salt. Add to the egg mixture and cook over boiling water until slightly thickened, stirring constantly. Cool until partially set. Fold in sour cream and green onions. Pour into a 1 1/2 quart ring mold and chill until set.

Optional: Marinate zucchini and cauliflower in dressing. Unmold salad, fill center with vegetables and garnish with watercress, parsley or salad greens. Goes well with ham or corned beef. Serves 12.

OVEN ROASTED VEGETABLES

Dorinda Torrance

6 large potatoes, scrubbed, cut
  into 3/4 inch chunks
6 large carrots, peeled, cut into
  1/2 inch chunks
2 Tbsp vegetable oil
2 Tbsp all purpose flour
2 Tbsp cornstarch
1 Tbsp salt
2 tsp granulated sugar

1 Tbsp dried parsley flakes
1 1/2 tsp garlic powder
1 tsp each onion powder,
  thyme, dried dill weed
3/4 tsp each rosemary and
  paprika
1/4 tsp each dry mustard and
  ground white pepper
Cooking spray

Heat oven to 400°F. Place potato and carrot chunks in a large bowl. Toss with vegetable oil until well coated. Set aside. Blend together flour, cornstarch, salt, sugar, parsley, garlic powder, onion powder, thyme, dill weed, rosemary, paprika, mustard and pepper. Toss herb mixture with potatoes and carrots. Line a large shallow pan with foil and generously spray with cooking spray. Place coated vegetables on prepared pan. Bake in oven for 30 minutes or until vegetables are tender.

CAULIFLOWER SANDWICHES

Inger-Lise Koetke

1 cup cauliflower, steamed and
  mashed
1 to 2 Tbsp mayonnaise
1/4 tsp prepared mustard
1/4 tsp mixed salt and pepper
2 Tbsp chopped celery or water
  chestnuts

1/2 cup shredded lettuce or
  sprouts
1 tsp shredded carrots
Grated cheese
Sandwich bread

Mix well. Make sandwich and butter outside. Cook like a grilled cheese sandwich.

ASPARAGUS PILAF WITH ARTICHOKES

Marge Gale

1 Tbsp oil
1 medium yellow onion, diced
8 to 10 white mushrooms,
  chopped
2 large cloves garlic, minced
1 1/2 cups long grain rice
  (white or brown)
3 1/2 cups water or vegetable
  broth
14 oz can artichoke hearts,
  rinsed and coarsely chopped

10 to 12 asparagus spears
  (fresh), trimmed and cut into
  1 inch pieces
1/4 cup chopped fresh parsley
1 1/2 tsp curry powder
1/2 tsp black pepper
1/2 tsp salt or sea salt
Juice of 1 or 2 lemons
  (optional)

In a medium saucepan, heat the oil. Add the onions, mushrooms and garlic, stirring for about 5 minutes. Stir in the rice, water, artichokes, asparagus, parsley, curry powder, pepper and salt and bring to a simmer over medium-high heat. Stir, cover and cook over medium-low heat until rice is tender, 15 to 20 minutes. Fluff the rice and let stand for 5 to 10 minutes before serving. If desired, squeeze the lemon juice over the pilaf.

*We do not stop playing because we are
old; we grow old because we stop playing.*

TOASTED ORZO PILAF

Sandy Taylor

1 Tbsp butter or margarine
1/4 cup chopped onion
1 clove garlic, minced
1 cup uncooked orzo pasta
1/4 cup white wine, water or
  chicken broth
3 cups warm water, divided

3/4 tsp salt
1/2 tsp dried marjoram
1/4 tsp pepper
3/4 cup packaged shredded
  carrots, chopped
Fresh parsley, chopped

In large nonstick skillet, melt butter, over medium heat. Add onion and garlic and cook 1 minute. Add orzo and cook for 1 to 2 minutes, stirring until coated and lightly browned. Add wine (water or chicken broth), 2 cups warm water, salt, marjoram and pepper. Cook for 8 to 10 minutes, stirring occasionally, until liquid is almost absorbed. Add carrots and remaining water. Cook for 5 to 6 minutes, stirring often, until liquid is absorbed and orzo is tender. Transfer to serving bowl. Sprinkle with parsley, if desired. Makes 6 servings.

THE RICE DISH

Dorinda Torrance

2 boxes Uncle Ben's long grain
  and wild rice mix
1 Tbsp olive oil
1/2 cup mayonnaise
2 1/2 Tbsp liquid honey
2 Tbsp lemon juice
2 tsp cider vinegar
1/4 cup parsley, chopped

1/4 cup green onion, thinly
  sliced
1/4 tsp salt
1/4 tsp pepper
1/4 lb red and green grapes (or
  more)
1 cup almond pieces, toasted

Cook rice, as package directs. Toss with oil to coat. Separate grains of rice if they stick together (a fork works well). Let cool then cover and refrigerate (lasts 3 days).

Mix mayonnaise, honey, lemon juice and vinegar until smooth. Stir in parsley, green onion, salt and pepper. Refrigerate in tightly covered jar. Add grapes and almonds and dressing to rice prior to serving.

Character is much easier kept than recovered.

WILD RICE WITH
MUSHROOMS AND ALMONDS

Gretchen Hopkins

1 cup uncooked wild rice
3 Tbsp butter
1/2 cup slivered almonds
2 Tbsp snipped chives or
   chopped green onions

8 oz can mushroom stems and
   pieces, drained
3 cups chicken broth

Wash and drain rice. Melt butter in large skillet. Add rice, almonds, chives and mushrooms; cook and stir until almonds are golden brown, about 20 minutes.

Pour rice mixture into ungreased 1 1/2 quart casserole. Heat chicken broth to boiling; stir into rice mixture. Cover tightly; bake at 325°F for about 1 1/2 hours or until all liquid is absorbed and rice is tender and fluffy.

HAZELNUT WILD RICE

Sandy Taylor

1 cup golden raisins
1/2 cup dry sherry
4 1/2 cups chicken broth
1 cup uncooked wild rice,
   rinsed and drained
1 cup uncooked brown rice
3 Tbsp butter, divided

1 cup coarsely chopped
   hazelnuts, almonds or
   pecans
1/2 cup chopped fresh parsley
1/2 tsp salt
1/4 tsp pepper

In a small saucepan, bring raisins and sherry to a boil over medium heat. Simmer for 5 minutes. Cover. Remove from heat. Set aside.

In 4 quart saucepan, combine broth, rices and 2 tablespoons butter. Bring to a boil over high heat. Cover. Reduce heat to medium-low. Simmer for 35 to 45 minutes, or until rice is tender and broth is absorbed. Meanwhile, melt remaining tablespoon of butter in skillet over medium heat. Add nuts and sauté for 4 to 5 minutes, or until toasted. Add raisins with sherry, toasted nuts, parsley, salt, and pepper to cooked rice just before serving.

Sight is a faculty; seeing is an art.

TABBOULEH

Margot Hollaway

1/2 cup fine-grain bulghur
   wheat, rinsed and drained
1/3 cup fresh lemon juice
1/3 cup olive oil
Salt, to taste
1/8 tsp cayenne powder

2 cups minced parsley
2 Tbsp fresh mint leaves,
   minced
4 green onions, diced
2 tomatoes, halved, seeded and
   diced small

Mix bulghur wheat with lemon juice and set aside for 30 minutes. Mix oil, salt, and cayenne. Mix bulghur, parsley, mint, onions and tomatoes and combine with dressing. Cover and refrigerate for 2 hours.

POTATO CASSEROLE

Dolly Des Rochers

1 large bag hash browns
Salt and pepper, to taste
1/2 cup chopped onion
1 can Campbell's cream of
   celery soup

1 small sour cream
2 cups grated cheddar cheese
1/2 cup melted butter
1 1/2 cups crushed corn flakes

Empty hash browns in a casserole dish. Add salt and pepper to taste. In bowl mix onion, soup, sour cream and grated cheese. Pour over hash browns. Top with melted butter and corn flakes. Bake at 350°F for 1 1/2 hours.

GREEK LEMON POTATOES

Wendy Ternowesky

6 potatoes, sliced or chunks
1/4 cup olive oil
Salt and pepper
1 chicken bouillon cube

1 cup hot water
1 fresh lemon
Parsley

Place potatoes in 9x13 inch pan or casserole dish. Mix all of the above. Pour over the potatoes. Cover and bake for 1 hour at 350°F. Remove cover and cook 10 minutes longer to absorb some of the liquid.

It is the hard jobs that make us.

POTATOES FLORENTINE

Ann Bishop

6 large potatoes, cooked and
  mashed
1/4 cup butter
2 eggs
1/4 cup Parmesan cheese

Salt, pepper and nutmeg, to
  taste
10 oz frozen chopped spinach,
  thawed and drained

Whip potatoes, butter, eggs, cheese and spices together. Fold in spinach. Pour into greased casserole dish. Bake at 350°F for 45 minutes. Top with additional cheese.

NEW POTATOES WITH ROSEMARY

Cathy Guarasci

1 lb small new potatoes, boiled
3 Tbsp light olive oil
1 Tbsp tarragon vinegar
1 tsp Dijon mustard

1 Tbsp anchovy paste
1 clove garlic, minced
1 tsp fresh rosemary or
  oregano

Toss with warm potatoes.

GREEK POTATOES

Cathy Guarasci

8 to 10 medium potatoes
1 cup water
1/2 cup lemon juice
1/3 cup olive oil

3 cloves garlic, minced
2 tsp salt (less if you wish)
2 tsp oregano
1 tsp pepper

Cut potatoes into thick chunks. Arrange in a 9x13 inch pan. Mix ingredients together and pour liquid over potatoes. Bake uncovered at 325°F for 2 hours.

*There is nothing so annoying as to have two
people go right on talking when you're interrupting.*

MAKE-AHEAD GARLIC
MASHED POTATOES

Maureen Cockburn

6 medium potatoes (2 1/4 lb),
  scrubbed
3 cloves garlic, peeled
1/4 cup sour cream
4 green onions, chopped

Salt and pepper, to taste
2 Tbsp each dry bread crumbs
  and grated Parmesan cheese
1 tsp butter, cut into small
  pieces

Cut potatoes into chunks and boil potatoes and garlic until tender. Drain well, return potatoes and garlic to saucepan. Place over low heat to dry out slightly, shaking saucepan occasionally. Remove from heat; add sour cream. Mash roughly with a fork. With electric mixer, beat potatoes until smooth and creamy. Stir in green onions and salt and pepper to taste. Spoon potatoes into a greased 8 cup baking dish. Don't smooth top too much, leave the texture slightly rough.

In small bowl, combine bread crumbs and Parmesan, sprinkle evenly over potatoes. Dot with butter. Bake covered in 350°F oven for 20 minutes. Remove lid, bake 10 to 15 minutes or until bubbly and golden brown on top. Serves 6.

MASHED POTATOES
WITH CORN & GARLIC

Dorinda Torrance

1 lb baking potatoes, peeled
  and cut up
1 Tbsp salt
1 Tbsp butter
2 cloves garlic, minced
1/2 tsp ground cumin

2 cups corn niblets, cut from
  approximately 4 ears
2 green onions, thinly sliced
2/3 cup milk or cream
1 tsp salt (or to taste)
1/4 tsp pepper

Boil potatoes until cooked. Drain water. Melt butter on low heat in medium sized skillet. Add garlic. Cook until fragrant. Add cumin and corn and cook 2 minutes. Add green onions, milk, salt and pepper. Bring to a boil and remove from heat. When potatoes are tender, drain well and mash. Stir in corn mixture. Add more hot milk if potatoes are too thick.

Habit can be your best friend, or your worst enemy.

MAKE-AHEAD MASHED POTATOES   *Dorinda Torrance*

3 lb potatoes (Yukon Gold or russet) peeled and cut into 2 inch chunks
4 oz cream cheese
1/2 cup sour cream
1/2 cup hot milk
1/4 cup butter
1 Tbsp salt
2 Tbsp chopped fresh parsley
2 Tbsp chopped fresh chives
1 tsp paprika (preferably smoked)

Cook potatoes gently in a large pot of salted water until tender. Drain well. Return to hot pot and mash. Beat in cream cheese, sour cream, hot milk, butter, salt, parsley and chives. Taste and adjust if necessary. Pipe or swirl potatoes in serving size portions in a baking dish. Sprinkle with paprika. Refrigerate up to 2 days. Reheat in a preheated 350°F oven for 45 to 50 minutes until thoroughly hot.

EXTRA RECIPES

Main Dishes

TIMETABLE FOR ROASTING MEAT AND POULTRY AT 325 °F

— Roast uncovered with no liquid added.

— Times are approximate; for accurate results use a meat thermometer.

	Ready to Cook Weight (lbs.)	Approximate Time Required to Roast (hours)	Internal Temperature (°Fahrenheit)
Beef roasts	4-6	2-2½ (rare)	140°
		2½-3½ (medium)	150°
		2¾-4 (well done)	170°
Veal roasts	3-5	2-3½ (well done)	180°
Lamb roasts	3-5	2-3 (medium)	145°
		2¼-3¼ (well done)	170°
Pork loin roasts	4-6	2¼-3½ (well done)	180°
		3½-4 (well done)	185°
Ham, cook before eating	5-7	2½-3½	170°
Ham, fully cooked	2-7	1½-2	130°
Chicken broilers or fryers, stuffed	1½-2½	1-2*	185°
	2½-4½	2-3½	
Turkey roasters, stuffed	8-12	3½-4½*	185°
	12-16	4½-5½	
	16-20	5½-6½	
	20-24	6½-7	

.*Poultry without stuffing may take less time.

COOKING GUIDE FOR EGG, MILK, MEAT AND CHEESE DISHES

	Oven Temperature (°Fahrenheit)	Approximate Time Required for Baking (Minutes)
Souffles	350° - 375°	30 - 60
Macaroni and Cheese	350° - 375°	25 - 45
Lasagne	350° - 375°	30 - 45
Meatloaf	350°	60 - 90
Meat Pie	400°	25 - 30
Casseroles	350° - 375°	25 - 40
Scalloped Potatoes	350°	50 - 60
Quiche	375° - 400°	35 - 45
Pizza	400° - 425°	20 - 30

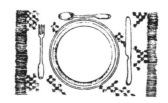

MAIN DISHES

CASSEROLES

ROASTED NUT LOAF

Dorinda Torrance

2 1/2 cups roasted unsalted
    nuts (try cashews, peanuts,
    or mixed nuts)
1/2 lb cottage cheese
1 onion, finely chopped
2/3 cup grated cheddar cheese
2/3 cup grated Parmesan
    cheese
2 1/2 cups fresh whole wheat
    bread crumbs

1 carrot, grated
1 clove garlic, crushed
1/4 cup fresh parsley, chopped
2 eggs, beaten
3 tsp sweet chili sauce (or
    ketchup)
3 tsp soy sauce
Freshly ground black pepper

Finely chop the nuts and combine with the cottage cheese, onion, cheese, bread crumbs, carrot, garlic, and parsley in a bowl and mix well. Add eggs, chili sauce, soy sauce, pepper, and mix thoroughly. Press the mixture into a well-greased loaf pan, approximately 9x4x6 inches. Bake in a preheated 350°F oven for 40 to 45 minutes, until loaf is cooked and firm to touch. Allow to stand in the pan for 15 minutes before removing. This loaf can be served hot or cold. Cut into slices and serve.

CARROT PECAN CASSEROLE

Barb Bayles

3 lb carrots, sliced
2 eggs, slightly beaten
2/3 cup sugar
3 Tbsp flour
1/2 cup soft butter
1 Tbsp grated orange rind

1/2 cup chopped pecans,
    toasted
1 tsp vanilla
1/4 cup milk
1/4 tsp ground nutmeg

Cook carrots until tender; drain and let cool slightly. Process in food processor until smooth. Transfer carrots to large mixing bowl and stir in remaining ingredients. Spoon into lightly greased 11x7 inch baking dish (can be covered and chilled for up to 8 hours at his point). Bake casserole, uncovered, at 350°F for 40 minutes.

BEAN POT

Gretchen Hopkins

2 (15 oz) cans kidney beans
with sauce
2 (15 oz) cans deep brown
beans with sauce
2 (15 oz) cans lima beans,
drained

1/2 lb bacon fried and
crumbled
2 large onions, sliced,
quartered and fried
1 cup ketchup
3/4 cup brown sugar
1/4 cup vinegar

Mix together. Heat on stove top or bake at 350°F for 45 minutes. Can be frozen.

PORK AND RICE BAKE

Dolly Des Rochers

1 1/2 cups uncooked rice
28 oz can tomatoes
1/2 cup chopped green pepper
1 tsp salt
1 tsp chili powder
2 dashes pepper

6 pork chops
Salt and pepper, to taste
1 medium onion, cut in rings
1/2 cup grated cheddar cheese
1/2 green pepper, cut in rings

Place uncooked rice, tomatoes, green pepper, salt, chili powder and pepper in a large casserole dish. Break up larger pieces of tomato. Arrange 6 pork chops on top of rice mixture and sprinkle with salt and pepper. Place onion rings on top of chops and bake at 350°F for 1 1/4 to 1 1/2 hours. Remove foil and sprinkle with cheddar cheese, place a ring of green pepper on top of each chop and return to oven for 10 to 15 minutes longer.

Adolescence: the age when children try to bring up their parents.

CHILI AND CHIPS

Sandy Taylor

2 lb lean ground beef
1 cup chopped onion
2 cans (14 1/2 oz each) diced
   tomatoes with green chilies
15 1/4 oz can kidney beans,
   drained, rinsed
6 oz can tomato paste

1 Tbsp chili powder
1 1/4 tsp salt
1/4 cup shredded Mexican
   cheese blend
Sour cream, cilantro and tortilla
   chips (optional)

In pot over medium-high heat, crumble in beef; stir in onion and garlic. Cook, stirring often, until browned. Drain. Add next 5 ingredients. Increase heat to high; bring to boil. Reduce heat to medium; simmer, stirring occasionally for 20 minutes. To serve, transfer to bread bowl or plate. Sprinkle with cheese. Garnish with sour cream, and cilantro if desired. Serve with chips. Makes 8 (1 cup) servings.

FAMILY FAVORITE SHEPHERD'S PIE

1 lb lean ground beef, pork or
   lamb, or a combination of
   these
2 medium onions, chopped
2 large cloves garlic, minced
1 carrot, minced
1/3 cup tomato paste

2/3 cup water
1 tsp dried thyme
1 Tbsp Worcestershire sauce
Salt and freshly ground pepper,
   to taste
2 cups mashed potatoes
Dash paprika

In skillet over medium heat, cook meat, stirring to break up meat, until brown. Pour off fat. Add onions, garlic, and carrot; cook until tender. Add tomato paste, water, thyme, Worcestershire sauce, salt, and pepper to taste. Simmer for 5 minutes, stirring up any brown bits on the bottom of the pan. Spoon meat mixture into an 8 cup (2 L) baking or microwave-safe dish; spread mashed potatoes evenly on top. Sprinkle with paprika to taste. Bake in 375°F oven for 35 minutes or until heated through, or microwave at high power for 9 minutes.

*There is only one pretty child in
the world, and every mother has it.*

MOUSSAKA

Kathryn Waldie

2 eggplants or medium
  zucchini
1/2 tsp salt
1 kg ground lamb or lean beef
1 Tbsp butter
Salt and pepper, to taste
2 medium onions, chopped
2 garlic cloves, crushed
1/4 tsp cinnamon
1/4 tsp nutmeg
2 Tbsp parsley

8 oz tomato sauce
1/3 cup red wine
4 Tbsp butter
4 Tbsp flour
1 cup milk
1 cup whipping cream
3 egg yolks, beaten
Salt and pepper, to taste
2 Tbsp olive oil
500 g Monterey Jack cheese,
  grated

Cut eggplant into 1/4 inch slices, sprinkle with salt and set aside. Sauté ground meat in butter with salt and pepper, onions, garlic, cinnamon, nutmeg, parsley, and tomato sauce. Add wine and simmer for 20 minutes, stirring occasionally.

To make Béchamel sauce, melt butter and stir in flour. Gradually add milk and cream, stirring constantly until mixture thickens. Add egg yolks in a slow stream, away from heat and stirring constantly. Return to heat and simmer for 2 to 3 minutes longer. Remove from heat and season with salt and pepper.

Wipe eggplant dry and quickly brown in olive oil. Set on paper towel to drain. In greased 9x13 inch pan, place a layer of eggplant, then cover with meat sauce, sprinkle with 1/3 of the cheese, cover with remaining eggplant, sprinkle with 1/3 of the cheese, cover with Béchamel sauce and top with remaining cheese. Bake at 350°F for 1 hour. Serves 6 to 8.

When opportunity knocks, some people are in the backyard looking for four-leaf clovers.

MEATBALL STEW
Dorothy Cunningham

Meatballs, browned (at least 18)
1 large onion, chopped
4 cloves garlic, minced
2 1/2 cups mushrooms (halved)
2 tsp dried basil
3/4 tsp dried sage
1/4 tsp hot pepper flakes
4 tsp flour
1 1/2 cups beef broth or stock –
3 Tbsp tomato paste
1 Tbsp red wine vinegar
1 bay leaf
3 carrots, sliced
1/2 tsp salt
1 sweet red pepper, diced
1 sweet yellow pepper, diced
1 zucchini, halved and sliced
1 cup frozen peas
Pepper, to taste

Drain all but 1 tablespoon fat from the meatballs and set balls aside. Add onion, garlic, mushrooms, basil, sage, and pepper flakes to the remaining oil in the pot and cook, stirring for about 3 minutes. Sprinkle with flour, and stir and cook for 1 minute. Gradually pour in stock, scraping browned bits from bottom of pan. Bring to a boil. Stir in tomato paste, vinegar, bay leaf, carrots, salt and meatballs. Simmer, partially covered for 20 to 30 minutes. Stir in peppers and cook 1 minute. Add zucchini and peas, simmer for 5 to 10 minutes. Season to taste and serve over pasta. Serves 8. Freezes well.

FIVE HOUR STEW
Susan Moreau

2 lb lean stewing beef
1 1/2 cups V8 or tomato juice
2 Tbsp Minit Tapioca
1 1/2 tsp salt
2 tsp Lang's beef dip mix
2 cups potatoes, cut into pieces
2 cups carrots, cut into pieces
2 cups celery, cut into pieces
1 onion, sliced
2 cups peas (optional)

Grease roaster or large casserole. Combine all ingredients, except peas. Bake at 275°F for 3 to 5 hours. When 1/2 hour of baking time is left, add peas. Serves 6.

All you need to grow fine vigorous grass is a crack in the sidewalk.

BEEF STEW WITH COGNAC
AND HORSERADISH MUSTARD

Audrey Karpoff

3 Tbsp olive oil
1/2 lb smoked bacon, cut in 1/2
  inch pieces
2 large sweet onions, chopped
2 shallots, chopped
2 garlic cloves, minced
3 Tbsp flour
Salt and pepper, to taste
2 lb beef chuck
1/2 cup cognac
3 cups beef broth
1 cup chopped Italian plum
  tomatoes

1 dry bay leaf
4 branches thyme
1/2 cup horseradish
1/2 cup Dijon mustard
2 large carrots cut into 1 inch
  pieces
2 large parsnips, cut into 1 inch
  pieces
1/2 lb Crimini mushrooms,
  sliced
1/4 cup red wine

Cook bacon in oil until crisp. Drain. Cook onions and shallots until golden (15 minutes). Add garlic, cook 1 minute. Using slotted spoon transfer to a bowl. Combine flour, salt and pepper, toss in beef and brown in batches until brown. Add oil if necessary. Place beef in bowl with onion mixtures. Add cognac to the pot and scrape up brown bits. Stir in broth, tomatoes, bay leaf, thyme, and mustard. Mix well. Return meat and onion to the pot, reduce heat and simmer for 2 hours until meat is tender. Add carrots and parsnips, cover and simmer for 45 minutes. Sauté mushrooms in oil in another pan until brown. Stir mushrooms and red wine into stew. Simmer an additional 10 minutes. Serve with green salad.

STANDBY STEW

Sandy Taylor

1 lb stewing beef, cut in chunks
1 to 2 potatoes, cut in chunks
7 1/2 oz can tomato sauce
1 cup water or red wine
1 large onion, chopped

1 to 2 carrots, sliced
5 oz beef broth or boulllon
1 tsp thyme
Salt and pepper, to taste

Put everything into a large heavy pot with tight fitting lid. Bake at 300°F for 4 hours, until meat is very tender.

BEST EVER MEAT LOAF

Marianne Routley

2 eggs
2/3 cup milk
2 tsp salt
1/4 tsp pepper
3 slices crumbled bread
1 onion, chopped

1/2 cup shredded carrots
1 cup shredded cheese
1 1/2 lb lean ground beef
1/4 cup brown sugar
1/4 cup catsup
1 Tbsp prepared mustard

Preheat oven to 350°F. Beat 2 eggs lightly in large mixing bowl. Add milk, salt, pepper, crumbled bread and beat until the bread disintegrates. Add onion, carrots, cheese and ground beef and mix well. Pack into 5x9 inch loaf pan. Mix brown sugar, catsup and prepared mustard and spread mixture over the meat loaf. Bake for approximately 1 hour. Serves 4 to 6.

HAM CASSEROLE

Mary Krysko

12 eggs
Salt and pepper, to taste
5 to 6 drops Tabasco
1 lb Monterey Jack cheese,
  shredded

2 cups cubed cooked ham,
  sautéed
1 pt cream cottage cheese
1/2 cup flour
1 tsp baking powder
1/4 cup butter or margarine

Beat eggs with salt and pepper. Add Tabasco, stir in flour, baking powder, ham, both cheeses and butter or margarine. Pour mixture into well greased 9x13 inch pan and bake in 400°F oven for 15 minutes. Turn oven down to 350°F and bake 15 minutes longer or until crust is golden brown.

No cowboy was ever a faster draw than a grandmother pulling baby pictures out of her purse.

TOMATO BROCCOLI QUICHE
Sandy Taylor

1 pastry shell
1 large onion, chopped
1/2 cup sliced mushrooms
1/2 tsp oregano
2 Tbsp butter
8 bacon slices, diced
1/2 cup grated Parmesan
  cheese
1 small pkg cream cheese

1 cup milk
3 eggs, beaten
1 cup broccoli, cooked and
  chopped
1/2 cup soft bread crumbs
3/4 tsp salt
1/4 tsp pepper
4 tomatoes, sliced

Sauté onions, mushrooms and seasonings in butter. Crisply fry strips of bacon, drain and crumble. Cream together cheeses, blend in milk and beaten eggs. Fold in broccoli, bacon, bread, onion, and mushrooms. Pour into shell. Arrange tomato slices on top. Bake at 425°F for 10 minutes, then at 350°F for 25 minutes. Let stand 10 minutes before serving.

SPINACH PIE
Jane Girard

Oil to brown onions
1 bunch green onions, finely
  chopped
2 (10 oz) pkg chopped frozen
  spinach
2 cups creamed cottage
  cheese

1 lb feta cheese, broken into
  chunks
6 beaten eggs
Salt, pepper and dill weed, to
  taste
1/2 cup melted butter
10 to 12 sheets of filo pastry

Brown onions and add spinach, which has been thawed, drained and moisture squeezed out. Mix eggs, cottage cheese, feta cheese and spices together. Combine the two mixtures. Using a brush and the melted butter, butter a 10x13 inch pan. Place a sheet of filo in pan and butter, layer on another piece of filo and butter. Use at least five layers. Pour in spinach mixture and turn sides of dough in. Cover with another five layers of butter filo dough. With a sharp knife, make a cut through the top layers. Sprinkle a little water on top and bake for 1 hour at 350°F.

Those who complain most are most to be complained of.

CLASSY CHICKEN

Dolly Des Rochers

3 skinless chicken breasts
1/2 tsp pepper
1/2 cup Best Foods
  mayonnaise
1 tsp lemon juice

10 oz fresh or frozen, broccoli,
  asparagus or peas
10 oz can cream of chicken
  soup
1 tsp curry powder
1 cup grated cheese

Cut chicken into 2x4 inch pieces and sprinkle with pepper, sauté slowly until white. Drain. Cook veggies until just soft enough for a fork to go through, drain. Arrange veggies on bottom of buttered casserole dish. Place chicken on top. Mix soup, mayonnaise, curry, and lemon together. Pour over chicken. Sprinkle with cheese. Bake uncovered at 375°F for 30 to 35 minutes.

CHEESY CHICKEN ENCHILADAS

Gail Zbuk

1 lb boneless, skinless, chicken
  breast halves, cut into 1/2
  inch pieces
1 envelope taco seasoning
16 oz jar chunky salsa
15 oz can black beans, rinsed
  and drained

2 cups Sargento Mexican blend
  shredded cheese, divided
15 oz can mild enchilada
  sauce, divided
8 (6 inch) flour tortillas
2 Tbsp sliced ripe olives

Prepare chicken with taco seasoning as directed on package of taco seasoning mix; cool 10 minutes. Stir in salsa, beans, corn and 1 cup cheese. Spread 1/4 cup enchilada sauce on bottom of a 13x9x2 inch baking dish. Place 2/3 cup chicken mixture down center of each tortilla; roll up. Place in dish, seam side down, on top of sauce. Pour remaining enchilada sauce over tortillas; sprinkle with remaining cheese and the sliced ripe olives. Bake at 375°F for 20 minutes or until cheese is melted and filling is hot. Yield: 8 servings.

One nice thing about egotists:
they don't talk about other people.

ROAST CHICKEN DINNER POT PIE   *Maureen Cockburn*

3 to 6 lb (2.5 to 3 kg) roasting
  chicken
3 Tbsp olive oil
Salt and pepper, to taste
4 unpeeled red potatoes, cut
  into 1 inch cubes
1/2 lb small mushrooms
1/2 lb mini carrots
10 oz pkg pearl onions, peeled

2 1/2 cups chicken stock
1 tsp each dried sage,
  marjoram and thyme
2 Tbsp cornstarch
1/4 cup whipping cream
2 cups frozen peas
Half pkg (397 g) frozen half puff
  pastry, thawed
1 egg

Remove any fat from inside chicken. Place chicken in large shallow roasting pan. Drizzle 1 tablespoon of the oil over chicken, sprinkle with salt and pepper. Roast uncovered in 400°F oven for 40 minutes. Add potatoes, mushrooms, carrots and onions to pan in single layer. Drizzle vegetables with remaining oil, sprinkle with salt and pepper and stir to coat well. Roast for 30 to 40 minutes or until the vegetables are tender and the chicken juices run clear when thickest part of thigh is pierced. Remove chicken and set aside.

With slotted spoon, remove vegetables to large bowl, leaving pan juices in the roasting pan. When cool enough to handle, remove chicken meat from the bones and cut into bit-size pieces, discard skin and bones. Add chicken meat to vegetable bowl. Skim any excess fat from pan drippings. Add 2 cups of stock, sage, marjoram and thyme. Bring to boil, scraping up any brown bits. Dissolve cornstarch in remaining stock; add to pan and cook, stirring until thickened. Remove from heat, stir in cream and peas and combine with chicken mixture. Taste and adjust seasoning. Spoon into greased 9x13 inch baking dish. Let cool. Roll out dough and place over chicken mixture. Bake in 400°F oven for about 1/2 hour.

CHICKEN-RICE AND
GREEN BEAN CASSEROLE   *Maureen Cockburn*

2 1/4 cups cooked rice
2 cups cooked and seasoned
  green beans
1 cup milk
10 oz can condensed cream
  of chicken soup

1 tsp salt
1/4 tsp pepper
1 cup grated nippy cheddar
Paprika

Mix together all ingredients except the cheese. Pour into a well greased 2 quart casserole or individual casseroles. Sprinkle cheese over the top. Sprinkle well with paprika. Bake in moderate 350°F oven for 35 to 40 minutes. Serve hot. Makes 8 servings. Other cream soups can be substituted for cream of chicken.

SOUTHWESTERN CHICKEN CHILI   *Dorothy Cunningham*

2 1/2 lb chicken pieces, skinned, boneless and cut into bite size pieces
2 Tbsp margarine, divided
4 medium carrots, sliced
2 medium onions, chopped
2 garlic cloves, minced
4 tsp chili powder
1 tsp cumin
1/2 tsp oregano
1/4 tsp salt
Pinch pepper
28 oz can crushed tomatoes, undrained
3 Tbsp tomato paste
2 Tbsp lime juice
1 can baby corn on the cob
1 tsp sugar
19 oz can chick peas, drained
19 oz can kidney beans, drained
3 stalks celery, sliced
1 sweet green pepper, diced
3 Tbsp coriander, divided
Tortilla chips and lime slices for garnish

Brown chicken pieces in 1 tablespoon margarine or oil, and remove. Add remaining margarine, carrots, onion, and garlic. Cook for 3 minutes, stirring constantly. Add chili powder, cumin, oregano, salt, and pepper. Cook for 1 minute. Add tomatoes, tomato paste, lime juice, corn, sugar, and chicken. Bring to a boil and simmer for 20 minutes. Add chick peas, kidney beans, celery, green pepper and 2 tablespoons coriander. Cover and simmer for 30 minutes. Season to taste. Garnish with lime slices and remaining coriander and tortilla chips. Good with baked potatoes or rice, and a salad. Serves 8 generously. Freezes very well.

STUFFED PEPPERS   *Dolly Des Rochers*

6 green peppers with either tops cut off or if large cut in half
1 cup rice, cooked
Salt, to taste
1 lb ground meat, cooked
1 medium onion, chopped and sautéed
1 can tomatoes, chopped
Garlic in 2 Tbsp butter
1/2 cup grated cheese or seasoned bread crumbs

Core peppers very carefully and cook in boiling water for 5 minutes and drain. Sprinkle with salt and let cool. In a bowl mix meat, rice, onion, garlic, tomatoes, salt and pepper. Fill peppers with the mixture and bake for 20 minutes at 350°F. Cover with grated cheddar or seasoned bread crumbs. Raise temperature to 400°F and brown.

TAMALE PIE

Maureen Cockburn

1 cup cornmeal	2 tsp chili powder
1 tsp salt	2 tsp salt
3 cups boiling water	2 cups canned tomatoes,
2 Tbsp butter	drained
1 clove garlic, minced	1 cup canned corn
1 lb ground beef	1/2 cup chopped ripe olives

Add cornmeal and salt to rapidly boiling water. Simmer for 10 minutes. Line bottom and sides of a greased 1 1/2 quart casserole with 3/4 of the mixture. Place in 350°F oven for 15 minutes. Melt butter, add garlic, onions and ground beef and brown. Add remaining ingredients. Mix well. Pour into casserole. Pat remaining cornmeal on top in strips. Bake for 45 minutes. Serves 6. Serve with Waldorf salad and buttered toast.

ITALIAN POT ROAST AND NOODLES

Cathy Guarasci

3 lb lean chuck or rump roast,	1 tsp salt
or stewing beef	1/4 tsp black pepper
2 Tbsp oil	1/2 tsp sugar
2 cloves crushed garlic or 1/4	1 large tin tomato sauce
tsp garlic powder	3 cups water
2 medium onions, chopped	1 lb noodles
1 1/2 tsp oregano leaves	Grated Parmesan or Romano
1 tsp whole thyme	cheese
1/2 tsp basil leaves	Chopped chives or green onion
1/8 tsp cinnamon	or peppers to top

Brown all sides of meat slowly in oil. Remove meat and lower heat. Add garlic and next 8 seasonings to the oil in the pot. Simmer for 5 minutes, stirring. Return meat to pan. Mix tomato sauce with water and pour over meat. Bring to full boil. Lower heat and cover loosely. Simmer slowly for 2 to 3 hours turning meat occasionally. When meat is tender, cook noodles and drain. Slice the roast and arrange with noodles and cover with sauce. Sprinkle with cheese and chives. Makes 6 servings.

One person with courage makes a majority.

CHINESE NOODLE CASSEROLE
Sandy Taylor

1 lb ground beef, browned and
   drained
1 large onion, chopped
1 stalk celery, chopped
10 oz can mushrooms

10 oz can tomato soup
1 Tbsp chili powder
1 green pepper
2 cups dry Chinese noodles

Brown ground beef, onions, and celery. Add drained mushrooms, tomato soup, chili powder and green peppers. Mix ingredients together and then mix in 1 1/2 cups of noodles. Place mixture in casserole dish and top with remaining dry noodles. Bake at 325°F for 1 1/2 hours.

PASTA PUTANESCA
Paula Watkin

2 large cans diced tomatoes,
   drained
1/4 cup extra virgin olive oil
8 anchovy fillets, roughly
   chopped
1/4 tsp hot pepper flakes, to
   taste
1 tsp oregano

1/2 cup small black olives,
   sliced
1/4 cup drained capers
4 cloves garlic, peeled and
   chopped finely
1/2 cup chopped Italian parsley
Grated Parmesan

This sauce will cook almost as fast as fresh pasta, so if you are using dried, you need to start it before the sauce. Bring the tomatoes and olive oil to a boil. Keep the sauce at a full boil and add the rest of the ingredients, one by one, stirring after each addition. Reduce the heat slightly and boil briefly until sauce is slightly thickened. Serve over hot pasta and top with grated Parmesan. Serve with green and white fettuccini. Don't be afraid of the anchovies, they mostly add salt.

Sympathizing with a person is like patting a
dog on the head - they both follow you for more.

SEAFOOD LASAGNA

Patricia McKinnon

8 lasagna noodles
2 Tbsp butter
1 cup chopped onion
8 oz pkg cream cheese, softened
1 1/2 cups creamed cottage cheese
1 egg, beaten
2 tsp dried basil
1/2 tsp salt
1/8 tsp pepper
2 (10 oz) cans cream of mushroom soup
1/3 cup milk
1/3 cup dry white wine or dry vermouth
5 oz can crab
1 lb shelled, deveined cooked shrimp
1/4 cup grated Parmesan cheese
1/2 cup shredded sharp cheddar cheese

Cook noodles. Place 4 in a 9x13 inch pan. Cook onion in butter. Add cream cheese, cottage cheese, egg, basil, salt and pepper. Spread 1/2 of mixture over noodles. Combine soup, milk and wine. Stir in crab and shrimp. Spoon 1/2 of mixture over cheese layer. Repeat all layers. Sprinkle with Parmesan cheese and bake uncovered at 350°F for 45 minutes. Top with sharp cheddar cheese, brown under broiler and let stand 15 minutes before serving.

EASY CHEESE LASAGNA

Alyson Clifton

1 jar spaghetti sauce
6 uncooked lasagna noodles
15 oz container fat-free ricotta cheese
1 to 2 cups raw vegetables (mushrooms, broccoli, bell peppers), sliced or chopped
1/2 pkg frozen spinach, thawed and well drained
8 oz pkg shredded low-fat mozzarella cheese

Preheat oven to 375°F. Spray 11x7 inch baking dish with non-stick cooking spray. Spread 1/3 of the sauce on bottom of the dish. Arrange 3 noodles in a single layer over sauce. Top with another 1/3 of the sauce. Mix ricotta cheese and spinach together and spread over sauce. Put veggies on top and sprinkle with 1/2 of the mozzarella cheese, then remaining noodles in a single layer. Spread evenly with remaining sauce. Cover dish with foil; bake until noodles are tender and mixture is piping hot, about 1 hour. Sprinkle with remaining mozzarella cheese. Bake uncovered for 5 minutes longer. Let stand 5 minutes before serving. Serves 6.

MUSHROOM LASAGNA

Kathryn Waldie

3 Tbsp olive oil
1 small onion, finely chopped
1 clove garlic, minced
1 stalk celery, finely chopped
3/4 lb mushrooms, thinly sliced
1/2 sweet red pepper, finely chopped
2 cups canned plum tomatoes
1/2 tsp dried thyme
1/2 tsp dried oregano
1/2 tsp dried basil
Salt and pepper, to taste
4 lasagna noodles
1 1/2 cups cottage cheese
1 1/2 cups shredded mozzarella cheese
1/4 cup freshly grated Parmesan cheese

In saucepan, heat oil over medium heat. Cook onion, garlic and celery for 3 minutes or until onion is softened. Stir in mushrooms and red pepper; cook, stirring occasionally, for 5 minutes or until liquid has evaporated. Add tomatoes, thyme, oregano and basil; bring to boil. Reduce heat and simmer uncovered for 15 to 20 minutes or until thickened. Season with salt and pepper to taste.

In a large saucepan of lightly salted boiling water, cook noodles until tender. Drain and rinse under cold water. Spread on damp tea towel. Spread one-quarter of the mushroom mixture in an 8 inch square baking dish. Top with layer of noodles, cutting to fit dish and using ends to fill in spaces. Spread with half of the cottage cheese; sprinkle with half of the mozzarella. Spread another quarter of the mushroom mixture over top. Repeat layering with remaining ingredients, ending with mushroom mixture. Sprinkle with Parmesan. Bake in 350°F oven for 35 minutes or until heated through and bubbling around sides. Makes about 6 servings.

LAZY LASAGNA

Alyson Clifton

1 lb ground beef
1 jar seasoned pasta sauce
1/2 pkg broad egg noodles
8 oz mozzarella cheese, grated
1/3 cup sour cream
1/2 cup Parmesan cheese, grated

Preheat oven to 350°F. Grease 2 L lasagna dish. Cook meat until browned, drain off fat, stir in pasta sauce, simmer uncovered over medium-low heat for 10 minutes, stirring often. Meanwhile, cook noodles until tender but firm, drain well. Combine grated mozzarella cheese with sour cream. In bottom of dish, spread half the noodles. Layer the cheese mixture then half the meat mixture, the remaining noodles and remaining meat. Sprinkle with Parmesan cheese. Cover and bake for approximately 20 minutes, or until hot and bubbly. Remove cover and cook 5 minutes more.

VEGETARIAN LASAGNA

Lorraine Giordano

4 cups tomato sauce
2 tsp garlic powder
2 tsp oregano
2 tsp basil
1 cup sliced mushrooms
2 cups frozen spinach, thawed
  and drained

3 oz shredded mozzarella
  cheese
9 oz cooked lasagna noodles
6 oz firm tofu
2/3 cup 1% cottage cheese
2 Tbsp Parmesan cheese
2 egg whites

In a saucepan, combine 1 1/3 cups tomato sauce and spices. Boil, and then simmer for 5 minutes. Stir in mushrooms. In a bowl, combine remaining ingredients except mozzarella and lasagna noodles. Spread 1 1/3 cups tomato sauce on bottom of 13x9 inch pan, arrange half of the noodles on top. Spread spinach mixture evenly over noodles. Spread 1 1/3 cups sauce on top. Top with remaining noodles and mozzarella cheese. Bake at 350°F until cheese is slightly brown, approximately 30 to 40 minutes.

MEATLESS LASAGNE

Sandy Taylor

5 to 6 lasagna noodles
10 oz frozen spinach, thawed
  and juice squeezed out
1 cup grated mozzarella cheese
1 1/3 cups dry cottage cheese
1/4 tsp ground nutmeg
2 Tbsp salad oil

1/2 tsp salt
1/2 tsp pepper
1 tsp sugar
1 large onion, chopped
1/2 tsp oregano
15 oz can tomato sauce

Cook noodles, rinse and drain. Mix spinach, 3/4 cheese, cottage cheese, oil, salt, pepper, sugar, onion, and oregano. Grease an 8x8 inch pan. Layer noodles, then cheese and spinach mixture (pat down hard), then tomato sauce, noodles and rest of tomato sauce. Sprinkle remaining cheese on top. Cook in preheated oven at 350°F for 45 to 50 minutes until thoroughly hot.

Vacation: the period when those rainy
days for which a person saves usually arrive.

CRUSTLESS CRAB QUICHE BAKE
Gretchen Hopkins

8 eggs, beaten
2 cups half-and-half cream
1 large sweet red pepper,
  chopped
8 oz pkg imitation crabmeat,
  chopped
1/2 cup soft breadcrumbs
  (fresh)

1 1/2 cups shredded Swiss
  cheese
1 1/2 cups shredded cheddar
  cheese
1/2 cup chopped green onions
1 tsp salt
1/2 tsp pepper

In a large bowl, combine all ingredients. Transfer to a greased 13x9x2 inch baking dish. Bake, uncovered at 350°F for 1 hour or until a knife inserted near the center comes out clean. Let stand for 10 minutes before serving.

NANCY REAGAN'S CRABMEAT CASSEROLE
Vi Sakaki

1 lb 4 oz can artichoke hearts
1 lb crabmeat
1/2 lb fresh mushrooms,
  sautéed
4 Tbsp butter
2 1/2 Tbsp flour
1 cup cream

1/2 tsp salt
1 tsp Worcestershire sauce
1/4 cup dry medium sherry
Paprika, cayenne and pepper,
  to taste
1/4 cup grated Parmesan
  cheese

Place artichokes in bottom of greased baking dish. Spread a layer of crabmeat over. Add a layer of sautéed mushrooms. Melt butter in saucepan. Add remaining ingredients, except cheese. Stir well after each addition to form a smooth sauce. Pour sauce over artichoke-crab layers and sprinkle cheese on top. Bake at 375°F for 20 minutes.

SALMON FETTUCCINI
Cathy Guarasci

3 cloves garlic, minced
1 small onion
1 pt cherry tomatoes, halved
1/2 cup chicken broth
1 Tbsp cornstarch
2 cups cooked salmon chunks

1/4 cup lemon juice
2 Tbsp chopped fresh basil
1 Tbsp each capers and lemon
  zest
1/4 tsp black pepper
8 oz fettucine, cooked

In fry pan, sprayed with cooking oil, sauté garlic and onions for 4 minutes. Add tomatoes, cook 1 minute. Combine broth and cornstarch. Bring to boil stirring, boil 1 more minute. Add next 6 ingredients. Stir until heated through. Serve over the pasta with Parmesan or Romano cheese.

SALMON LUNCHEON DISH

2 tomatoes
1 small onion, cut finely
213 g tin salmon, boned and
  skinned
2 eggs, beaten

3/4 cup milk
1/2 cup dry breadcrumbs
1 cup grated cheese
Salt, pepper, parsley, to taste

Preheat oven to 350°F. Grease dish. Cut tomatoes and layer in bottom of dish. Sprinkle with breadcrumbs. Spread the onion over, then spread the fish over. Beat egg and milk, add salt, pepper and parsley, pour over fish. Cover with grated cheese. Cook in oven for 30 to 40 minutes.

SEAFOOD & BROCCOLI RICE   *Linda Baker*

1/2 cup chopped onion
2 cups sliced mushrooms
1 Tbsp butter
2 cups hot cooked rice
2 cups cooked seafood (or
  shrimp, scallops, chicken,
  turkey)
3 cups chopped steamed
  broccoli

1 cup chopped snow peas or
  peppers or both
2 chopped green onions
10 3/4 oz cream of mushroom
  soup
1/2 cup shredded cheddar
  cheese

Steam vegetables until tender. Stir butter into warm rice then stir in vegetables, seafood and soup (undiluted). Put into casserole dish. Top with cheese and bake at 350°F for 20 minutes.

SPAGHETTI WITH SEAFOOD   *Lorna Ruthman*

1/4 cup olive oil
2 cloves garlic, minced
1/4 tsp crushed chili pepper
8 oz scallops, cut up
8 oz shrimp, shelled, deveined
  and cut up
1/4 cup chopped parsley,
  divided

1 lb spaghetti, cooked
1/3 cup Italian flavored bread
  crumbs (process old bread
  and add Italian seasoning
  and Parmesan cheese)
Salt and freshly ground pepper,
  to taste

Heat oil and cook garlic and chili pepper over medium heat until fragrant, about 1 to 2 minutes. Add seafood and half the parsley, cooking 2 to 3 minutes longer. Combine seafood mixture, spaghetti, bread crumbs and remaining parsley and mix well. Season with salt and pepper and serve hot.

TUNA CASHEW CASSEROLE
Sandy Taylor

4 oz can chow mein noodles
1 can cream mushroom soup,
  undiluted
1/4 cup water
7 1/2 oz can (1 cup) tuna,
  chunk style

1/4 lb salted cashews
1 cup celery, finely diced
1/4 cup onion, minced
Pepper and salt, to taste

Reserve 1/2 cup noodles. Toss all other ingredients together and place in a 1 1/2 quart casserole. Sprinkle remaining noodles on top. Bake for 30 minutes in 325°F oven.

TOFU NUTLOAF OR
ALSO CALLED TOFURKEY
Sieglinde Holmes

1 large onion, chopped
1 garlic clove, pressed through
  a garlic press
2 Tbsp butter
1 lb tofu crumbled, well drained
1 cup mixed nuts, finely
  chopped (peanuts, almonds,
  filberts, etc.)
1 cup brown rice, cooked
1 cup dry bread crumbs
2 eggs
A few dashes Tamari and
  Worcestershire sauce

3 Tbsp melted butter
1 Tbsp sage (this is important)
1/2 tsp thyme
1/2 tsp marjoram
Salt and pepper, to taste
Brewer's Yeast Gravy:
1/2 cup yeast flakes
1/4 cup flour
1/3 cup oil
Water
2 to 3 tsp Tamari
Salt and pepper

Sauté onions and garlic in butter until soft. Combine the rest of the ingredients. Add a little water if it is too crumbly. Top with melted butter and bread crumbs, mixed. Bake for 30 minutes at 350°F. For Tofurkey add some dried cranberries and shape into a loaf and serve with cranberry sauce.

Brewer's Yeast Gravy: Toast yeast and flour in a small saucepan until just lightly browned. Add the oil and stir while it bubbles and turns golden brown. Add water slowly to make gravy. Stir in Tamari and salt and pepper to taste. Serves 6 to 8.

TOFU CHILI

Cathy Guarasci

2 chopped onions
4 to 5 cloves garlic, chopped
2 to 3 stalks celery, chopped
Block of solid tofu, grated or
    diced
Rosemary, thyme, salt and
    pepper
Chili powder
1 or 2 Tbsp Worcestershire
    sauce
Parsley

2 or 3 carrots, chopped
Tin pinto beans
Tin kidney beans
1 cup lentils
1 or 2 chopped medium
    zucchini
2 tins canned tomatoes
1 tin tomato paste
1 eggplant, chopped
1 or 2 medium potatoes

Sauté, onion, garlic, celery, zucchini, eggplant, potatoes and tofu, in olive oil. Add spices to suit your taste. A lot of chili powder is good. Add all the other ingredients, bring to a boil. Partially cover and simmer for about 2 hours, or until well cooked. Serve over rice.

MEAT

CRANBERRY MEAT BALLS

Alyson Clifton

1 box Swedish meatballs
1 bottle chili sauce

1 can whole cranberry sauce
1 Tbsp brown sugar

Preheat oven to 350°F. In a large oven proof bowl, mix chili sauce, cranberry sauce and sugar together. Add meatballs and mix well. Bake for 1 hour or until meatballs are heated through and sauce has thickened.

*The person who rows the boat
doesn't have time to rock it.*

SWEDISH MEATBALLS

Carol Swaykoski

1 lb lean ground beef
1/2 lb ground pork
1/2 cup minced onion
3/4 cup dry bread crumbs
1 Tbsp snipped fresh parsley
2 tsp salt
1/8 tsp pepper
1 tsp Worcestershire sauce
1 egg

1/2 cup milk
1/4 cup salad oil
1/4 cup flour
1 tsp paprika
1/2 tsp salt
1/8 tsp pepper
2 cups water
3/4 cup sour cream

Mix thoroughly beef, pork, onion, bread crumbs, parsley, 2 teaspoons salt, 1/8 teaspoon pepper, Worcestershire sauce, egg and milk. Refrigerate for 2 hours. Shape mixture, by rounded tablespoons, into balls. In large skillet, slowly brown and cook meatballs in 1/4 cup oil. Remove meatballs, keep warm. Blend flour, paprika, 1/2 teaspoon salt, and 1/8 teaspoon pepper into oil in skillet. Cook over low heat, stirring until mixture is smooth and bubbly. Remove from heat, stir in water. Heat to boiling, stirring constantly. Boil and stir 1 minute. Reduce heat and gradually stir in sour cream, mixing until smooth. Make sure sauce has stopped boiling before adding sour cream or it may curdle. Add meatballs. Heat through.

WIENER SCHNITZEL

Audrey Karpoff

6 veal cutlets (about 4 oz)
  pounded thin
Salt and pepper
1 cup all purpose flour
2 eggs

2 cups dry bread crumbs
1/4 cup vegetable oil
6 sprigs fresh parsley
1 lemon, cut into 6 wedges
1 Tbsp butter, melted (optional)

Pat veal dry and season with salt and pepper. Place flour in a shallow dish. Beat eggs together lightly in another shallow dish and place bread crumbs in a third shallow dish. Dip seasoned veal into flour and shake off excess. Dip into egg to coat completely. Place in crumbs and pat crumbs into both sides. If not cooking right away, refrigerate in a single layer. Just before serving, heat oil in a large skillet. Cook cutlets in oil, in batches, a few minutes per side until browned. Place on serving plate with parsley. Drizzle with butter and serve with lemon wedges. Makes 6 servings.

GRILLED SIRLOIN OR
FLANK STEAK & MARINADE
Pat Johnston

1 1/2 lb thick sirloin or flank
   steak
1/4 cup low sodium soy sauce

1/4 cup orange juice
2 cloves garlic, chopped
1 Tbsp ginger, grated

Leave steak whole or cut into serving pieces. Mix marinade of soy sauce, orange juice, garlic and ginger. Add to steak and marinate for 30 minutes to 2 hours. Remove from marinade and grill meat to desired temperature.

MARINATED ROAST BEEF
Maureen Cockburn

4 lb beef tip, heel or round or
   rolled rump roast
1 1/2 cups beer or apple cider
1/3 cup vegetable oil
1 tsp salt

1/4 tsp garlic powder
1/4 tsp pepper
1/4 cup cold water
2 Tbsp flour
2 tsp instant beef bouillon

Prick beef roast thoroughly with fork. Place beef in deep glass bowl. Mix beer, oil, salt, garlic powder and pepper, pour on beef. Cover and refrigerate, turning occasionally, at least 12 hours. Place beef fat side up on rack in shallow pan. Reserve 1 cup of the marinade. Insert thermometer so tip is in center of thickest part of beef and does not rest in fat. Roast uncovered in 325°F oven until thermometer registers 160°F, about 3 hours.

Remove beef to warm platter. Heat reserved marinade over medium heat until hot. Shake water, flour and instant bouillon in covered container, stir gradually into marinade. Heat to boiling, stirring constantly. Boil and stir for 1 minute. Serve gravy with beef. Yield: 14 servings.

*When you begin to coast you
know you're on the downgrade.*

ROAST FILLET OF BEEF WITH
CORNICHON TARRAGON SAUCE

Audrey Karpoff

3 trimmed 3 1/2 lb fillets of
  beef, tied, at room
  temperature
1/3 cup olive oil
2 sticks (1 cup) unsalted butter,
  softened
2/3 cup Dijon mustard
1 1/4 cups minced shallots

5 cups dry white wine
1/2 cup minced fresh tarragon
  leaves or 2 Tbsp dried
1/3 cup heavy cream
40 cornichons (French sour
  gherkins) cut into julienne
  strips (about 1 cup)

Rub the fillets with oil, season with salt and pepper. In large roasting pan, leaving space between the fillets, roast them in preheated 550°F oven for 23 minutes, or until meat thermometer registers 130°F, for medium-rare meat. Transfer fillets to a platter and let them stand, covered loosely with foil for 15 minutes. In a bowl, with an electric mixer, cream together the butter and the mustard.

In a large saucepan combine the shallots, the wine and the tarragon and cook the mixture over moderately high heat until the wine is reduced to about 1 cup. (The mustard butter and the shallots mixture may be made 1 day in advance and kept covered and chilled. Reheat the shallots mixture before continuing if made the day before.) Add the cream and the cornichons, reduce the heat to low, and whisk in the mustard butter, a little at a time, and any meat juices that have accumulated on the platter. Season the sauce with salt and pepper and keep it warm, but do not let it boil. Slice fillets and serve with sauce. Serves 18.

GLAZED PORK TENDERLOINS

Dorinda Torrance

2 (1 lb) pork tenderloins
1/3 cup molasses
1/3 cup reduced-sodium soy
  sauce

2 Tbsp honey
2 Tbsp Worcestershire sauce

Trim tenderloins of excess fat. Combine the molasses, soy sauce, honey, and Worcestershire sauce in a shallow dish with the tenderloins. Cover and refrigerate several hours or overnight, turning several times. Grill pork over medium hot grill for about 20 minutes or until internal temperature is 160°F. To prepare in oven, bake at 350°F for about 50 minutes. Serves 8.

BRAISED BEEF SHORT RIBS
Audrey Karpoff

3 lb (1.5 kg) boneless beef
  short ribs
2 Tbsp olive oil
2 onions, chopped
3 cloves garlic, finely chopped
1 tsp dried rosemary or thyme
1 tsp salt

1/2 tsp freshly ground pepper
1 1/2 cups beef stock
1 cup canned tomatoes
  including juice, chopped
2 Tbsp Worcestershire sauce
3 strips orange peel (3 inches
  in length)

Pat meat dry with paper towels. In a Dutch oven or large saucepan, heat 1 tablespoon of the oil over medium-high heat and brown ribs in batches until browned on all sides. Add more oil as needed. Transfer to a plate when browned. Lower heat to medium and cook onions, garlic, rosemary, salt and pepper. Stir often, for 5 minutes, or until softened. Add stock, tomatoes and juice, Worcestershire sauce and orange peel. Return beef and any of its juices to the pan, bring it to a boil, cover and reduce heat so mixture simmers for 2 hours, or until meat is tender. Add more stock to keep meat just covered as it cooks.

PORK ROAST WITH
PEPPERCORN SAUCE
Sandy Taylor

4 lb (1.75 kg) pork top loin
  roast
1 Tbsp olive oil
1 tsp salt
1/2 tsp freshly ground pepper
Sauce:
1 Tbsp butter

1/3 cup finely chopped shallots
1/3 cup brandy
2 Tbsp green peppercorns in
  brine, drained
2 cups heavy cream
1/2 tsp salt

Heat oven to 350°F. Rub roast with olive oil. Sprinkle evenly with salt and pepper all over. Place roast on rack in roasting pan. Roast for 50 minutes to 1 hour, or until internal temperature of roast is 145°F (63°C). Tent roast with foil. Let stand 10 minutes. While roast stands, make sauce.

Sauce: Melt butter in large skillet over medium heat. Add shallots and sauté for 3 to 4 minutes, or until tender. Add brandy. Reduce for 2 to 3 minutes, or until brandy is nearly gone. Add peppercorns and mash slightly with fork. Add cream. Simmer sauce for 4 to 5 minutes, or until reduced to a sauce like thickness, whisking occasionally. Stir in salt. Serve sauce with roast. Yield: 8 to 10 servings.

PORK TENDERLOIN PARMESAN
Cindy Walter

1 pork tenderloin, any size
1 egg, beaten with 1 Tbsp
  water
1 cup dry bread crumbs
3 Tbsp Parmesan cheese
Olive oil, to coat fry pan
6 Tbsp mozzarella cheese

3 cloves garlic, minced
1 onion, minced
28 oz can tomatoes, diced
1 small can tomato paste
1 1/4 tsp salt
1/4 tsp pepper
1/4 tsp thyme

Tomato Sauce: Sauté garlic cloves and onion in 3 tablespoons olive oil. Add canned tomatoes, salt and pepper. Simmer uncovered for 10 minutes and then add tomato paste and thyme. Simmer for 20 minutes.

Cut the tenderloin in half vertically and pound till even thickness. Cut into 4 1/2x2 1/2 inch strips. Dip into egg mix then combination of bread crumbs and grated Parmesan cheese. Sauté tenderloin in olive oil until golden. Place in baking dish, slice or grate mozzarella cheese and put on top of each strip. Pour 2/3 of the tomato sauce over meat, then more mozzarella, then the balance of the tomato sauce. Sprinkle with Parmesan and bake at 350°F for 30 minutes.

BALSAMIC HONEY TENDERLOIN
Gail Zbuk

Marinade:
2 Tbsp liquid honey
2 Tbsp grainy mustard
2 Tbsp balsamic vinegar

1 Tbsp olive oil
1 garlic clove, minced
Salt and pepper, to taste
2 pork tenderloins

Marinade: In a large bowl combine ingredients.

Add pork to marinade and turn to coat. Marinate in refrigerator for up to 24 hours. Remove pork from the marinade and reserve liquid. Place pork on greased grill over medium-high heat. Brush with marinade. Close lid and cook, turning and basting occasionally, for about 18 minutes, or until inside has just a hint of pink. Transfer pork to cutting board and let sit for 5 minutes. Cut into 1/3 inch thick slices.

A bore is a person who puts his feat in his mouth.

ROAST PORK LOIN WITH PEACHES
Audrey Karpoff

3 lb pork loin
1 acorn squash, peeled and
  cubed
2 fennel bulbs, trimmed and
  cubed
6 cloves garlic (whole)
2 bay leaves

2 Tbsp olive oil
1/2 tsp thyme
1 cup apple cider/apple juice or
  white wine
2 peaches, peeled and
  quartered

Score meat and tie. In ovenproof pan sear meat in hot oil. Add salt, pepper and thyme. Remove meat from the pan. In the same pan, add butter or oil if necessary, brown acorn squash, fennel, garlic and bay leaves. Place pork loin on top of veggies. Add apple cider, juice or wine. Bake in 375°F oven for 1 to 1 1/2 hours. In the last 15 minutes of cooking, add peeled peaches.

PORK TENDERLOIN WITH SPICE RUB
& BALSAMIC CURRANTS
Kathryn Waldie

1 tsp ground cumin
1 tsp ground coriander seed
1/2 tsp ground cinnamon
Pinch cayenne
1 1/2 lb pork tenderloin,
  trimmed
2 Tbsp olive oil
Salt and pepper, to taste

1 tsp Dijon mustard
1/2 cup balsamic soaked
  currants
1 cup chicken stock
1 tsp fresh thyme leaves
2 tsp brown sugar or maple
  syrup (optional)

Combine the dry spices. Rub the tenderloin with 1 tablespoon of the olive oil and coat with the spices. Wrap in plastic wrap. Leave at least 20 minutes for some flavour to develop or prepare ahead and refrigerate for a more intense flavour. When ready to cook, preheat oven to 400°F. In an ovenproof skillet, heat the remaining olive oil until very hot. Unwrap the tenderloin and sear to create a nicely brown exterior. Season with salt and pepper. Place in the preheated oven for 15 minutes. Remove from the pan and wrap to keep warm. Drain off any excess fat from the skillet and add the Dijon mustard to the pan, whisking to incorporate any pan juices. Add the currants, chicken stock and thyme. Reduce over medium-high heat to a syrupy consistency. Taste and adjust the seasonings. For a sweeter sauce, add the sugar or syrup. When sauce has thickened, slice the pork and add any juice from the meat to the sauce. Serve drizzled with sauce and scatter the currants as garnish.

PULLED PORK-SOUTHERN
BARBEQUED PORK ROAST

Lorraine Giordano

2 tsp olive oil
1 onion, chopped
2 cloves garlic, minced or finely
  chopped
2 cups ketchup
1 cup cider vinegar
1 cup brown sugar

3 Tbsp Worcestershire sauce
1 tsp hot red pepper sauce
  (optional)
1 Tbsp Dijon mustard
3 lb boneless lean pork
  roast/loin
1 cup water

Heat oil in large saucepan. Add onion and garlic and cook until tender. Add ketchup, vinegar, sugar, Worcestershire, hot pepper sauce, mustard, and water. Bring to a boil. Simmer for about 20 minutes, stirring often, as sauce will reduce and thicken. Rub pork with 1 cup of prepared sauce. Place in a roasting pan, add 1 cup of water, cover, and cook in preheated oven for 3 hours at 325°F (160°C). After 3 hours of cooking, remove roast from pan, skim fat from juices in pan. Add remainder of sauce to defatted juices. Pull any visible fat off pork and dispose. Take two forks and pull the pork apart, so it looks shredded, and then add to sauce. Cover and bake for 1 hour. This is great served on buns, mashed potatoes, rice, or even polenta.

BARBEQUED PORK LOIN

Vi Sakaki

3 to 5 lb pork shoulder or loin
10 oz can tomato soup
1/3 cup chopped onion
1/3 cup chopped celery
1 clove garlic, minced

2 Tbsp brown sugar
2 Tbsp Worcestershire sauce
2 Tbsp lemon juice
2 Tbsp Dijon mustard
4 drops hot red pepper sauce

Place loin of pork in shallow pan. Roast in moderately low oven, 325°F for about 45 minutes per pound. One hour before meat is done, pour off drippings. Combine rest of ingredients and pour over the meat. Continue roasting, basting often.

It is better to be small and shine
than to be great and cast a shadow.

PORK CUTLETS
Dolly Des Rochers

6 pork chops or cutlets
1 Tbsp sesame oil
1 small onion, chopped
3/4 tsp ginger
1 tsp lemon juice

2 cloves chopped garlic
1/4 cup white wine
1/4 cup honey
1 Tbsp brown sugar

Place pork in a roasting pan. Combine oil, onion, ginger, lemon juice and garlic and marinate until ready to cook. When ready to cook, combine wine, honey and brown sugar. Pour marinade over pork and cook at 350°F for 45 minutes reserving some marinade to serve at the table.

PORK BROCHETTES
Vi Sakaki

1 lb pork tenderloin
3 Tbsp lemon juice
1 Tbsp chopped fresh
   rosemary or 1/2 tsp dried
   rosemary

1 Tbsp Dijon mustard
1/3 cup olive oil

Cut pork into cubes of about 1 1/2 inches. Mix together lemon juice, rosemary, mustard and oil. Marinate meat for at least 15 minutes. Drain and reserve marinade. Thread cubes onto skewers (if using wooden ones, soak them in cold water first to avoid burning). Grill brochettes 10 to 12 minutes, turning every 2 to 3 minutes. Boil marinade and spread over pork. Good with steamed rice and grilled vegetables such as zucchini, peppers and eggplants.

PORK CHOPS WITH CRANBERRIES
Dorinda Torrance

4 pork chops, about 1 inch
   thick
Salt and freshly ground black
   pepper

1 cup whole cranberries, fresh
   or frozen
1/4 cup liquid honey
1/4 cup red wine or stock

Season chops lightly with salt and pepper. Arrange in 8 inch square or round baking dish, greased. In a small bowl, combine cranberries, honey, and wine. Stir well. Pour over chops. Cover with foil and bake in preheated 350°F oven for 45 minutes. Remove foil. Continue baking for 10 minutes or until meat is tender.

TOURTIÈRE (Pork Pie)

Maureen Cockburn

Pastry for 2 (9 inch)
   double-crust pies
1/4 lb salt pork, diced
1 small onion, chopped
1/2 clove garlic, crushed
3 lb shoulder pork, minced
2 tsp salt

2 Tbsp each of chopped celery
   leaves and parsley
1/8 tsp each, mace and chervil
Pinch cloves and cayenne
Half bay leaf
1 1/2 to 2 cups meat stock or
   bouillon

Sauté the salt pork until crisply browned. Add the onion and stir-fry until onion is transparent, then add remaining ingredients. Simmer, stirring occasionally until thickened, about 35 to 40 minutes. If you plan to serve the tourtière hot, crumble one or two slices of day-old French bread into it to absorb some juice and keep the meat from spreading when you cut the pie. Roll out pastry to line the pie pans. Add the meat mixture. Dampen the rims and roll out the top crust. Seal the edges and bake at 425°F for 15 minutes, reduce heat to 350°F and cook for another 40 minutes.

SPARERIBS

Mary Krysko

Baby back ribs
2 Tbsp lemon juice
1 onion, chopped
10 oz tomato soup
1/2 cup ketchup

1/4 cup vinegar
2 Tbsp brown sugar
1 tsp paprika
2 Tbsp Worcestershire sauce
1 Tbsp dry mustard

Cut baby back ribs into serving portions and put into roasting pan. Add lemon juice and onions. Bake until brown. Mix remaining ingredients and pour over ribs and bake, covered with foil, in 350°F oven for approximately 1 1/2 hours.

The grass may be greener on the other side, but it is just as hard to mow.

SWEET AND SOUR SPARE RIBS
Dolly Des Rochers

Salt, pepper and garlic, to taste
1 kg spare ribs
Water to cover
1 cup Heinz ketchup

Less than 1/4 cup vinegar
1/4 cup brown sugar
2 tsp salt
1 tsp celery seed

Put salt, pepper and garlic on cut up ribs. Place in baking dish and cover with water and bake at 350°F for 1 hour. Pour off water. Combine, ketchup, vinegar, brown sugar, salt and celery seed. Pour 1/2 of this mixture over ribs. Bake at 375°F uncovered for 1 hour. Pour remainder of mixture onto ribs and bake for another 20 to 25 minutes each side.

FARMER'S MARKET
SAUSAGES AND APPLES
Jane Girard

Olive oil
4 to 6 large sausages, such as
** savoury, turkey, Italian, etc.**
3 small onions
3 small firm apples, such as
** McIntosh or Royal Gala**

1/2 cup apple juice
1/4 cup apple jelly or hot
** pepper jelly**
2 Tbsp Dijon mustard
1 tsp dried basil leaves
Freshly ground black pepper

Prick sausages and cook in frying pan with a bit of olive oil for 5 to 7 minutes, until well browned all over. Cut onions and unpeeled apples into wedges and cook in same pan after removing sausages. Reduce heat and cook about 2 minutes. Return sausages to pan and add apple juice and jelly, basil, mustard and pepper, and cook all 10 minutes. Serve over cooked wide noodles. Might need more apple juice.

BAKED HAM WITH MAPLE GLAZE
Gail Zbuk

5 to 6 lb ham, bone-in
Whole cloves
2 cups orange juice

1/2 cup maple syrup
1/4 cup marmalade
2 Tbsp Dijon mustard

Preheat oven to 325°F. Using a sharp knife, remove skin from ham. Score fat diagonally in a diamond design. Stud top of ham with cloves. Place ham on a wire rack in a roasting pan lined with foil. Bake ham for 2 to 3 hours. Pour 1/4 cup of glaze over ham every half-hour or so.

Glaze: Combine orange juice, syrup, marmalade and mustard in a medium saucepan. Bring to a boil and simmer for 5 minutes, until well blended.

HONEY-GLAZED PORK
WITH WILTED GREENS

Audrey Karpoff

2 tsp Dijon mustard
3 1/2 Tbsp red wine vinegar
4 Tbsp honey (good quality, preferably raw)
1 large garlic clove, finely chopped
1 tsp coarsely chopped fresh rosemary
1 Tbsp plus 4 tsp olive oil

1 3/4 lb pork tenderloin (2) or ham or pork loin
3/4 tsp coarse salt
Freshly ground pepper
1 large fennel bulb, trimmed and sliced longwise into thin strips
1/2 head escarole, cut into 2 inch strips (optional)
1/2 lb spinach, washed well

Preheat oven to 375°F. In a small bowl, make glaze. Whisk together 1 teaspoon mustard, 2 tablespoons vinegar, 2 tablespoons honey, garlic, rosemary, and 2 teaspoons oil. Place pork tenderloins in a shallow baking dish; pour glaze over pork, turning to coat evenly. Sprinkle 1/2 teaspoon salt, season with pepper. Roast in oven, spooning glaze over pork occasionally until thickest part of pork reaches 155°F on an instant-read thermometer, 30 to 35 minutes. Remove from oven; let rest until pork reaches 160°F, about 10 minutes.

Meanwhile make vinaigrette in a small bowl. Combine remaining 2 tablespoons honey, 1 1/2 tablespoons vinegar and 1 teaspoon mustard. Whisk until honey is dissolved. Slowly whisk in 1 tablespoon oil until emulsified. Whisk in any accumulated cooking juices from baking dish, if desired. Heat, over medium-high heat in a 12-inch sauté pan, remaining 2 teaspoons of oil. Add fennel, escarole, spinach and a splash of water, cook until greens are slightly wilted, about 1 1/2 minutes. Add vinaigrette and remaining 1/4 teaspoon salt to pan, stirring just to coat greens, about 30 seconds. Remove from heat; divide among four serving plates. Slice pork about 1/2 inch thick; arrange alongside greens. Serve immediately.

Instruction may end in the classroom
but education ends only with life.

ROAST LAMB WITH PEPPERCORN CRUST

Paula Watkin

3 Tbsp crushed dried
   peppercorn mix (black, green
   and white or red)
1 Tbsp fresh chopped or 1 1/2
   tsp dried rosemary
1/2 cup fresh chopped or 1 1/2
   tsp dried mint

5 cloves garlic, crushed
1/2 cup raspberry vinegar
1/4 cup Chinese soy sauce
1/2 cup dry red wine
1 deboned, untied leg of lamb
   (about 5 lb)
2 Tbsp Dijon mustard

Preheat oven to 350°F. Combine 1 tablespoon of the crushed peppercorns, herbs, and liquids in a large Ziploc bag. Add leg of lamb and squeeze out any air. Marinate in a dish in the fridge for 8 hours, turning occasionally. Remove roast from marinade, reserve marinade. Roll and tie roast. Set the roast in a roasting pan and spread mustard over the roast. Pat the remaining 2 tablespoons of peppercorns into the mustard. Carefully pour the reserved marinade around, but not on, the roast.

Bake for 1 1/2 hours, (or 18 minutes per pound for medium rare) basting occasionally. Add water if necessary to prevent the pan from drying out. Let the roast stand for 15 minutes before carving. The pan juices are very piquant and need to be strained and thickened with cornstarch and a cup of lamb or beef stock.

POULTRY

EASY CHICKEN DIVAN

Audrey Karpoff

20 oz pkg frozen broccoli or 2
   bunches fresh broccoli
2 cups sliced cooked chicken
   or 3 chicken breasts, cooked
   and boned
2 cans cream of chicken soup,
   undiluted
1 cup mayonnaise or salad
   dressing

1 tsp lemon juice
1/2 tsp curry powder
1/2 cup shredded sharp cheese
1/2 cup soft bread crumbs
1 Tbsp butter or margarine,
   melted
Pimentos, cut in strips

Cook broccoli in boiling salted water until tender. Arrange stalks in greased 11 1/2x7 1/2x1 1/2 inch baking dish. Place chicken on top. Combine soup, mayonnaise, lemon juice and curry powder; pour over chicken. Sprinkle with cheese. Combine crumbs and butter, sprinkle over top. Bake at 350°F for 25 to 30 minutes, until thoroughly heated. Trim with pimento strips. Makes 6 to 8 servings.

CORDON BLEU ROULADE
Sandy Taylor

4 whole (unsplit) chicken breasts, boneless, skinless
4 pieces cheesecloth, single layer (16x12 inches)
1 to 2 Tbsp olive oil
2 cups shredded Gruyere or Swiss cheese
16 to 20 large leaves of spinach
8 oz deli-sliced smoked ham
Red Wine Sauce:
1 Tbsp olive oil

2/3 cup finely chopped shallots
2 Tbsp tomato paste
2 tsp minced garlic
1 cup dry red wine
1 1/2 cups beef broth
1 Tbsp cornstarch dissolved in 1 Tbsp water
1/2 tsp salt
1/4 tsp pepper
1 Tbsp butter (optional)

Heat oven to 350°F. Lay chicken breast out flat. Trim away any fat and discard. Trim off thick portions of breast. Use thick portions to fit between breast halves to level them and fill gaps. Soak cheesecloth in olive oil. Squeeze out cheesecloth and spread pieces on work surface. Sprinkle open chicken breasts evenly with cheese. Layer with a single layer of spinach leaves, then top with ham. Tightly roll up breasts from side to side, tucking in ends as you roll. Wrap rolled breasts tightly in prepared cheesecloth pieces. (Chicken breasts may be prepared to this point and refrigerated several hours before roasting.)

Arrange rolled chicken seam side down on rack in roasting pan. Roast for 45 minutes. Remove from oven and remove cheesecloth. Increase oven temperature to 450°F. Return breasts to oven. Roast for 15 to 20 minutes longer, until fully cooked. Remove from oven and cover with foil. Let stand 10 minutes before slicing. Slice rolled breasts crosswise. Serve with Red Wine Sauce.

Red Wine Sauce: Heat oil in saucepan, over medium heat. Add shallots and sauté for 3 to 4 minutes, until tender. Add tomato paste and garlic. Sauté for 2 minutes. Add wine, stirring to loosen any browned bits from bottom of pan. Let boil for 5 to 7 minutes, or until wine is reduced by half. Add broth and bring to a simmer. Whisk in cornstarch mixture. Cook for 1 to 2 minutes, or until thickened. Strain sauce through fine-mesh sieve. Stir in salt, pepper, and butter. Sauce may be made in advance, refrigerated, and then reheated.

The greatest remedy for anger is delay.

BAKED CHICKEN SUPREME

Norma Mills

8 single chicken breasts,
  skinned and deboned
1/2 cup plus 1 Tbsp shortening
1/2 to 1 clove garlic
1 tsp salt
1/2 cup onion, chopped

2 Tbsp flour
28 oz can chopped tomatoes
1 can mushrooms
1 cup sour cream
1/4 cup Parmesan cheese

Brown chicken in 1/2 cup hot shortening. Place chicken in casserole. Slice garlic and mash with salt. Cook in remaining shortening with onion until onion becomes transparent. Blend in flour, add tomatoes and heat to boiling. Remove from heat, add mushrooms and sour cream gradually, stirring vigorously. Add cheese. Mix thoroughly and pour sauce over browned chicken. Cover and bake at 325°F for at least 1 hour.

EASY YUMMY CHICKEN BREASTS

Dorothy Cunningham

1 can mushroom soup
1 pkg onion soup mix
1 cup sour cream

1 Tbsp lemon juice
1 tsp celery seed or dill weed
6 to 8 boneless chicken breasts

Mix top 5 ingredients together. In a large casserole, layer breasts with sauce between layers. Bake, covered at 350°F for 1 hour.

CHICKEN WITH PAPAYA AND CHUTNEY

Margot Hollaway

1/2 cup sliced almonds
3 Tbsp oil
3 chicken breasts, skinned,
  boned and split
1 large papaya
1 1/2 Tbsp lime juice

1/2 cup Major Grey's mango
  chutney, chopped
1/2 cup chicken broth
1 tsp cornstarch
1/2 tsp ground ginger
Hot cooked spinach as desired

In wok, stir hot oil and almonds until golden. Set nuts aside. Peel papaya and remove seeds. Cut into bite-sized pieces. Place in bowl with lime juice. Stir. In another bowl, stir together chutney, broth, cornstarch and ginger. Cut chicken into 1/2 inch wide strips. Add oil to wok if necessary, and stir-fry the chicken in 2 batches until no longer pink in center (about 5 minutes). Set aside. Add chutney mixture to hot chicken and stir 2 minutes. Add papaya and stir just until fruit is warm. Serve over spinach and sprinkle with almonds. Serves 6.

CRANBERRY CHICKEN

Susan Moreau

Chicken pieces thighs or
  breasts
2 tsp margarine
1/2 cup chopped onion
2 Tbsp margarine

1 can cranberry jelly
2/3 cup ketchup
1/3 cup brown sugar
2 Tbsp vinegar
1 tsp dried mustard

Bake chicken with margarine for 45 minutes at 375°F. Drain. Sauté onion in 2 tablespoons margarine. Stir in rest of ingredients. Boil uncovered for 15 minutes. Pour over chicken and bake for 30 minutes at 375°F. Turn several times.

ROAST CHICKEN BREASTS

Jacqueline Fassnacht

1/4 cup cilantro leaves and
  stems
2 Tbsp onion, diced
2 Tbsp chopped garlic
2 tsp crushed black
  peppercorns
4 skinless, boneless chicken
  breasts
1 Tbsp soya sauce

2 tsp water
1/2 tsp salt
1 cup honey
1/2 cup water
1/4 cup lime juice
1/4 cup rice vinegar
2 Tbsp minced garlic
2 Tbsp chili paste or hot sauce

Place the cilantro, onion, garlic, and peppercorns in a food processor and puree to a paste, or pound to a paste with a mortar and pestle. Combine the mixture with the chicken, soya sauce, water and salt and marinate for at least 30 minutes. Preheat oven to 400°F. Place the chicken on a baking sheet and roast for 15 to 20 minutes, depending on the size of the breasts.

In pan, bring all sauce ingredients, honey, water, lime juice, rice vinegar, garlic and chili paste, to a boil, then simmer for 20 minutes on low heat. Makes 2 cups. Spoon honey lime sauce over the chicken and serve.

*No matter what your lot in life
may be, build something on it.*

GOLDEN GLAZED CHICKEN
Donna Wisniowski

6 to 8 chicken breasts,
  boneless, skinless
1/4 cup butter
1/2 cup honey
1/4 cup hot prepared mustard

2 tsp mild prepared mustard
2 tsp lemon juice
2 tsp curry powder
1 tsp salt
1 small clove garlic, minced

Arrange chicken breasts in a single layer in a baking dish. In saucepan, melt butter, then add remaining ingredients, stirring until smooth. Pour over chicken and bake uncovered at 350°F for 45 minutes to 1 hour. Baste occasionally with pan juices.

Option: Spread 2 sliced onions in bottom of greased 9x13 inch glass baking dish, salt and pepper. Add chicken on top.

MOZZARELLA CHICKEN
Audrey Davies

2 to 3 boneless, skinless
  chicken breasts
2 eggs
2 cups tomato sauce
1/2 tsp oregano
1 tsp salt

1/4 tsp pepper
3/4 cup dry bread crumbs
1/4 cup oil
1 cup grated mozzarella cheese
1/2 cup Parmesan cheese

Pound chicken breasts until 1/4 inch thick. Dip the chicken pieces in beaten eggs. Roll the chicken in the bread crumbs. Fry in oil until lightly brown. Put chicken into a casserole dish. Add the spices to the tomato sauce and pour over the chicken. Sprinkle the cheeses on top. Bake at 350°F for 30 minutes.

Love doesn't make the world go round,
but it certainly makes the ride worthwhile.

CHICKEN SOUVLAKI
Wendy Ternowesky

1/2 cup olive oil
2 Tbsp parsley flakes
2 tsp oregano
1/2 tsp pepper
1/2 cup lemon juice
1 clove garlic, minced
1/4 tsp cumin

1 tsp salt
8 inch long wood skewers
6 boneless, skinless chicken
   breasts
President's Choice (TGTBT) fat
   free tzatziki

Mix marinade ingredients, first eight ingredients and shake well in large Ziploc bag. Cut chicken into large pieces. Add chicken to marinade and let sit 3 to 4 hours or overnight. Soak skewers in cold water for 30 minutes before using. Push chicken pieces onto skewers. Barbeque until juices run clear or until chicken is no longer pink inside. Serve with tzatziki. Increase amount of chicken if desired.

CHICKEN FILLED PATTY SHELLS
Sandy Taylor

6 patty shells
1/4 cup butter
1 cup mushrooms, sliced
1 apple, peeled, cored and
   chopped
1/2 cup celery, finely chopped
1/4 cup green pepper, chopped
1/4 cup flour

2 cups milk
1 Tbsp lemon juice
Salt, pepper
1/2 tsp curry powder
2 Tbsp mayonnaise
1/2 cup peas, frozen
3 cups chicken, cooked, diced

Melt butter in medium saucepan. Add mushrooms, celery, apple, and green pepper. Cook until tender, about 5 minutes. Remove from heat and stir in flour until blended. Place back on heat and gradually add milk, stirring constantly until thickens and comes to a boil. Add seasonings and lemon juice. Simmer for 2 to 3 minutes. Add mayonnaise, peas and chicken, heat through. Spoon into and over patty shells. Makes 6.

Worry never robs tomorrow of its sorrow,
it only saps today of its strength.

CHICKEN PARMESAN

Alyson Clifton

2 lb chicken pieces
1 egg
2 Tbsp water
1/2 cup flour

3/4 cup grated Parmesan
  cheese
Salt and pepper, to taste
1 tsp oregano
3 1/2 Tbsp melted butter

Wash chicken pieces. Beat egg and water in a shallow bowl. In another bowl, combine flour, 1/2 cup grated cheese, salt, pepper and oregano. Dip chicken into egg, then in flour and cheese mixture. Put chicken in 2 1/2 quart casserole, pour melted butter over it. Bake in a preheated oven at 400°F for 45 minutes, brushing occasionally with butter. Before serving, sprinkle with remaining Parmesan cheese. Serves 4.

YUMMY CHICKEN

Ann Bishop

1/4 cup flour
1 tsp salt
1/4 tsp pepper
Dash thyme
3 to 4 lb cut-up chicken
1/4 cup butter, melted

4 green onions, chopped
1/2 cup mushrooms, sliced
2 Tbsp lemon juice
1 tsp sugar
1 tsp salt
1/3 cup apple juice

Mix flour, salt, pepper and thyme in a plastic bag. Shake chicken to coat well. Brown chicken in butter and remove to casserole dish. Add green onions and mushrooms to frying pan. Cover and simmer for 3 minutes. Add to casserole dish. Mix lemon juice, sugar, salt and apple juice. Pour over chicken and bake at 325°F for 1 hour. Serves 6.

Before you put your foot down, be
sure you have a leg to stand on.

EASY CURRY
Lorna Ruthman

1/4 cup plus 2 Tbsp butter or
   margarine
1/2 cup minced onion
1 Tbsp curry powder (or curry,
   turmeric combo)
1/4 cup plus 2 Tbsp flour
1 1/2 tsp salt

1 1/2 tsp ground ginger
2 cups chicken broth
2 cups hot milk
4 cups cooked, cleaned shrimp
   or cut up chicken/turkey
   leftovers
1 tsp lemon juice

Melt butter over low heat in a heavy saucepan. Saute onion and curry powder in butter. Blend in flour and seasonings into melted butter mix and cook over low heat until mixture is smooth and bubbly; remove from heat. Stir in broth and then the milk. Bring all to a boil, stirring constantly. Boil 1 minute. Add shrimp/chicken or turkey and lemon juice. Heat and serve over rice. Good with relishes over; raisins, salted almonds, peanuts, pineapple chunks, shrimp sauce, chutney or the like.

YUMMY ROAST CHICKEN
Joan Gilbertson

1 whole chicken
1 tsp salt
1/4 tsp pepper
1 lemon, quartered
8 large garlic cloves, peeled
   and smashed with side of
   knife

3 fresh rosemary sprigs or 1
   Tbsp dried
1 1/2 lb red skinned potatoes,
   scrubbed and cut into 1 inch
   chunks
1/4 cup butter or margarine,
   melted

Preheat oven to 400°F. Remove giblets and neck. Rinse chicken under cold water; pat dry with paper towels. Sprinkle with salt and pepper. Place chicken in large, oiled roasting pan. Stuff cavity with lemon, garlic, and rosemary. Wash hands. Scatter potatoes around the chicken. Sprinkle with salt and pepper if you wish. Baste chicken and potatoes with butter. Roast, basting occasionally with pan juices, for 1 1/4 hours or until meat thermometer reads 180°F. Transfer chicken and potatoes to platter. Discard lemon, rosemary and garlic.

Optional: Skim off fat from pan juices, mash in garlic and serve the juices as gravy.

TURKEY CREOLE

Maureen Cockburn

2 Tbsp oil
1 stalk celery, chopped
1/2 green pepper, chopped
2 cloves garlic, chopped
2 Tbsp all purpose flour
2 cups canned tomatoes,
   drained and chopped
1 cup turkey stock or water

1/4 tsp cayenne pepper
1 bay leaf
1/2 tsp each, dried oregano
   and thyme
2 cups cooked and diced
   turkey
4 green onions, chopped
Salt and pepper, to taste

In large saucepan, over medium heat, heat oil until sizzling. Add celery, green pepper and garlic. Cook stirring until softened, about 5 minutes. Stir in flour and cook, stirring occasionally until golden brown, about 3 minutes. Add tomatoes, turkey stock, cayenne, bay leaf, oregano and thyme. Bring to boil. Turn heat to low and simmer for 20 minutes, stirring occasionally until thick. Stir in turkey and green onions. Simmer together for 5 minutes or until turkey is heated through. Remove bay leaf and discard. Taste and adjust seasoning with salt and pepper. Serves 6.

HONEY CURRY CHICKEN

Jackie Pawson

1 medium chicken, cut up
1/3 cup butter
1/2 cup honey

1/4 cup prepared mustard
2 tsp curry

Melt butter in pan, then mix in other ingredients. Place chicken in pan, meaty side down, make sure all meat is covered in sauce. Bake at 375°F for 1 hour. Turn after 3/4 hour.

*Humility is a strange thing - the minute
you think you've got it, you've lost it.*

TURKEY CAKES
Maureen Cockburn

2 cups cooked turkey, finely chopped
2 Tbsp butter
1 medium onion, finely chopped
1 cup dried bread crumbs
1/4 cup chopped fresh parsley
2 eggs, lightly beaten
1/2 tsp salt
1 Tbsp Dijon mustard
1 tsp Worcestershire sauce
1/4 tsp Tabasco sauce (optional)
Pepper, to taste

1/4 cup whipping cream or plain yogurt
1/4 cup all purpose flour
1/4 cup vegetable oil
Piquant Sauce:
1 cup mayonnaise
2 Tbsp chopped dill pickles
1 clove garlic, chopped
2 Tbsp chopped parsley
2 Tbsp chopped black olives
1/4 tsp Tabasco, or to taste
2 tsp lemon juice
Salt and pepper, to taste

Combine all Piquant Sauce ingredients. Makes 1 1/2 cups of sauce.

Heat butter until sizzling in medium frying pan. Add onion, sauté until softened, about 3 minutes. Remove from heat, stir in bread crumbs. Combine turkey, bread crumbs mixture, parsley, eggs, salt, Dijon mustard, Worcestershire sauce and pepper to taste in large bowl. Add enough cream to bind mixture together. Using about 1/4 cup mixture for each, form patties about 1 inch thick. Sprinkle flour on a plate and coat patties on both sides. Heat oil in large frying pan on medium heat. Add patties in batches and fry until brown on both sides and heated through, about 2 minutes per side. Serve with Piquant Sauce, cranberry sauce or lemon wedges.

SEAFOOD

SEA BASS
Dorinda Torrance

Sea Bass
Worcestershire sauce
Lemon juice

Salt and pepper
Clarified butter
Safflower oil

Choose your own quantities. Roll Sea Bass in 1/2 and 1/2 Worcestershire sauce and lemon juice. Sprinkle with salt and pepper. Dip in 1/2 and 1/2 clarified butter and safflower oil. Put in pan and bake in a preheated 400°F oven for approximately 15 minutes. It will crispen on the outside.

STUFFED ARCTIC CHAR

Patricia McKinnon

1 whole Arctic Char (5 lb) deboned
1 cup softened butter, plus more to rub on fish
1 large onion, chopped
4 stalks celery, chopped
1 large green pepper, chopped
Pimento (just to add some colour) sliced
Salt and pepper, to taste

Mix butter, onion, celery, green pepper, pimento, salt and pepper. Fill the fish cavity with mixture. Secure the fish by tying in several places with string. Rub generously with butter. Wrap in foil. Place in roasting pan on rack, add enough water to cover bottom of pan, not touching fish (add more water as needed throughout cooking time). Bake for 50 minutes at 350°F.

CEDAR PLANK SALMON

Kay MacCormack

1 cedar plank
2 lb salmon fillets
2 tsp sesame oil
2 to 3 cloves garlic, chopped
1 Tbsp fresh ginger
3 Tbsp brown sugar
1 tsp salt
1 tsp cumin
1/2 tsp pepper

Combine all ingredients except salmon fillets. Make slits in salmon fillets and rub mixture into fish. Place each fillet on a cedar plank and bake in oven at 400 to 425°F for 15 minutes. Serve with wild rice and green salad.

MARINATED SALMON

Dolly Des Rochers

2 Tbsp brown sugar
1/2 tsp garlic
3 Tbsp soya sauce
1 Tbsp lemon juice
1 1/2 lb salmon

Marinate salmon for about 1 hour. Cook for 10 minutes per each 1 inch thickness of fish.

Everything has its beauty but not everybody sees it.

ROLLED SOLE STUFFED WITH CRAB   *Patricia McKinnon*

2 Tbsp butter or margarine
4 Tbsp finely chopped shallots
8 oz lump crabmeat, picked
   over
1/2 cup fresh bread crumbs
   (about 1 slice bread)
1 Tbsp chopped fresh parsley
2 tsp fresh lemon juice
1/2 plus 1/8 tsp salt

1/8 tsp plus pinch ground black
   pepper
6 sole or flounder fillets (6 oz
   each)
14 to 16 oz can tomatoes,
   drained
1/4 cup heavy or whipping
   cream
1 tsp chopped fresh tarragon
   or parsley

Preheat oven to 400°F. Grease 13x9 inch baking dish. In nonstick 10 inch skillet, melt 1 tablespoon butter over medium heat. Add 2 tablespoons shallots and cook until tender, about 2 minutes. Transfer to medium bowl. Add meat, bread crumbs, parsley, lemon juice, 1/4 teaspoon and 1/8 teaspoon pepper; toss with fork until evenly coated. Sprinkle skinned side of sole fillets with 1/4 teaspoon salt. Spoon crabmeat mixture evenly over fillets. Roll up and place, seam side down, in prepared baking dish and cook until just opaque throughout, about 25 minutes.

Meanwhile, in blender, purée tomatoes until sauce. In same 10 inch skillet, melt remaining 1 tablespoon butter over medium heat. Add remaining 2 tablespoons shallots, cook until tender, about 2 minutes. Add pureed tomatoes, remaining 1/8 teaspoon salt, and remaining pinch of pepper. Increase heat to high and cook, stirring frequently, until moisture has almost evaporated, about 5 minutes. Stir in cream, heating to boiling. Remove from heat and stir in tarragon. With wide slotted spatula, transfer fish to warm serving plate. Stir any juices in baking dish into tomato sauce; spoon over fish. Makes 6 main dish servings.

*People who don't stand for
anything will fall for anything.*

LOBSTER

Jacqueline Fassnacht

5 1/2 oz butter
1/2 cup lemon juice
2 Tbsp chopped flat-leaf
(Italian) parsley leaves
1 small clove garlic, crushed

8 lobster tails in the shell
2 lemons, cut into wedges
Salt and freshly ground black
pepper, to taste

Melt the butter in a small saucepan over medium heat and cook it for 3 minutes or until it begins to brown. Watch carefully to make sure that it doesn't burn. Lower the heat, and cook the butter for another 2 minutes, or until it is a dark, golden brown. Remove the pan from the heat, add the lemon juice, parsley, and garlic, and season with salt and freshly ground black pepper.

Cut the lobster tails lengthways and remove the digestive tract, but leave the meat in the shell. Preheat the chargrill plate to medium direct heat and brush the exposed lobster meat with lots of the butter mixture. Cook the lobster tails, cut side down, on the chargrill plate for 6 minutes, then turn over and cook for another 3 to 5 minutes, or until the shells turn bright red. While the lobster is cooking, put the lemon wedges on the hottest part of the chargrill and cook them for 1 minute on each side, or until they are marked and heated through. Arrange the lobster on a serving plate and serve it with grilled lemon wedges and the rest of the warm brown butter as a dipping sauce. Delicious with a green salad and some crusty bread to soak up the juices. Serves 8.

POOR MAN'S LOBSTER

Ann Bishop

16 cups water
1/2 cup salt

3/4 cup sugar
Chunks of halibut

Bring all above to a full boil. Drop halibut chunks into water. When fish rises to surface it is cooked. Serve with melted butter.

If Columbus had turned back no one would have
blamed him. No one would have remembered him either.

THE ONLY BARBECUE SALMON *Sandy Taylor*

3 lb fresh whole salmon, deboned
6 large garlic cloves, minced fine
1 tsp salt
4 Tbsp fresh parsley, minced fine
2 Tbsp sun-dried tomatoes (packed in oil), minced fine
1/4 cup olive oil

Remove the belly and pin bones from the fillet. Crush and mince the garlic cloves. Sprinkle with the salt. Using a wide bladed knife, grind the garlic into a pulp. Combine the garlic, parsley, dried tomatoes and olive oil in a jar. Cover with a lid and shake well to blend all the ingredients. Refrigerate until ready to use.

With a sharp knife, cut two lengthwise slits in the salmon fillet, dividing the surface of the fish into thirds. Cut to the skin but do not cut through it. Spread half of the garlic mixture over the fillet and into the slits. Place the fish on a preheated barbecue over medium heat (350°F). Close the lid and grill for 15 minutes. Spread the remaining garlic mixture on the fillet. Close the lid, turn the temperature to high (400°F) and grill 10 more minutes.

Remove the fish from the barbecue by inserting a spatula between the skin and the flesh, so that you can lift the fillet but leave the skin on the grill. Serves 4 to 6.

SHRIMP WITH GREEN CHILI PESTO *Kathryn Waldie*

4 oz freshly grated Parmesan cheese (1 1/4 cups)
2 cloves garlic
6 mild green chilies, or 2 (4 oz) cans mild green chilies, drained, stems and seeds removed
1/2 cup pine nuts
1/2 cup parsley leaves
1/4 cup fresh cilantro leaves
3 Tbsp safflower oil
1 1/2 lb shrimp (26 to 30 per lb), shelled and deveined
Garnish with 5 whole green chilies, parsley or cilantro leaves

In the bowl of a food processor fitted with steel blades, process the cheese with the garlic until blended. Add the chilies, pine nuts, parsley, cilantro and 2 to 3 tablespoons oil and process to a smooth paste. Toss the shrimp in a bowl with the pesto, and refrigerate, covered for at least 1 hour. Preheat the oven to 350°F. Place the shrimp on a sheet pan and bake, uncovered for 15 to 20 minutes. Arrange the shrimp on a large platter and garnish. Serve warm or at room temperature.

EASY GOURMET
SCALLOPS AND SHRIMP

Dorothy Cunningham

1 lb (500 g) uncooked or
  cooked fresh or frozen
  shrimp, peeled and deveined
1/2 lb (250 g) large sea
  scallops (or smaller bay
  scallops)
1/4 cup dry sherry
1/2 cup water
1/4 cup teriyaki sauce

1 tsp granulated sugar
3 large garlic cloves, minced
2 tsp freshly grated ginger
1/4 tsp chili flakes (optional)
1 large yellow pepper
1 large red pepper
2 green onions
1 Tbsp cornstarch
1 tsp olive oil

If using frozen shrimp, do not thaw, rinse under cold running water until the ice crystals melt. Pat dry with paper towels. Pat scallops dry, and place on a fresh paper towel while preparing other ingredients. If using large scallops, quarter them as they seem huge with the shrimp.

In small bowl, stir sherry with water, teriyaki, sugar, garlic, ginger and chili flakes. Core and seed peppers, and cut into 1/2 inch wide bite-size strips. Thinly slice green onions and set aside.

Place scallops in a bowl and lightly sprinkle with cornstarch. Stir until evenly coated. Heat oil in large wide fry pan and set over high heat. Add coated scallops to hot pan, shaking off excess cornstarch. Cook until golden (1 to 2 minutes per side). Add shrimp to pan (if using cooked shrimp, fast-fry for 30 seconds; if using uncooked shrimp, stir-fry for 2 minutes).

Immediately add pepper strips, stir in sherry mixture. Stir frequently until shrimp are bright coral and peppers are tender crisp, 4 to 6 minutes more. Remove from heat and sprinkle with green onions. Serve over rice or noodles and drizzled with pan sauce. Yield: 4 to 6 servings.

Habits are like easy chairs - easy
to get into, hard to get out of.

GARLIC AND HERB-CRUSTED SALMON   *Sandy Taylor*

4 cups dry bread crumbs
1 Tbsp each, salt and pepper
1 Tbsp garlic, minced
6 Tbsp grated Parmesan
cheese
1 Tbsp each, fresh thyme and
parsley
1 Tbsp olive oil
3 Tbsp, minced red pepper
1 Tbsp tomato paste
2 Tbsp minced onion
Pinch cayenne pepper

1 tsp each, lemon and lime
juice
1/4 cup fish stock
Tiger prawns, butterflied, as
many as you like
16 oz fillets of salmon
Egg wash (1 egg beaten with 1
Tbsp water)
2 Tbsp olive oil
1 Tbsp butter
Chives for garnish

Heat olive oil in a sauté pan. Add onion, peppers, tomato, cayenne, salt and pepper to taste. Simmer 1 minute and then add lemon and lime juice. Add stock and boil until reduced by half. Add prawns and simmer for 2 minutes.

Combine bread crumbs, salt, pepper, Parmesan, garlic, thyme and parsley. Mix evenly and keep refrigerated. Dry off the salmon with a towel, brush with egg and press on garlic breadcrumb mixture. Pour 2 tablespoons olive oil and 1 tablespoon of butter in the sauté pan. When butter starts to brown, add salmon, crust-side down. Cook 2 minutes on each side and turn over. Finish in 450°F oven for 5 minutes. Place sauce on plate, lay salmon over sauce and top with prawns. Sprinkle with chopped chives and serve.

EXTRA RECIPES

Desserts

BAKING TEMPERATURES AND TIMES

Food	Oven Temperature (°Fahrenheit)	Approximate Time Required for Baking (Minutes)
Cakes		
Butter, cupcake	350°	15 - 25
layer	350°	20 - 35
loaf	350°	45 - 60
Fruit	275°	120 -300
Angel	375°	30 - 45
Sponge	350°	30 - 45
Cookies		
Drop	350° - 375°	8 - 15
Meringue	250°	50 - 60
		then turn off oven and cool
Rolled	350 - 375°	8 - 12
Squares	350 - 375°	20 - 35
Desserts		
Fruit Crisps	350° - 375°	35 - 45
Cheesecake	350°	45 - 60
Custard	350°	30 - 60
Pastry		
One crust pie (unbaked shell)	400° - 425°	30 - 40
Meringue on cooked filling in preheated shell	350° (or)425°	12 - 15 / 4 - 5
Shell only	450°	10 - 12
Two crust pie with uncooked filling	400° - 425°	45 - 55
Two crust pie with cooked filling	425° - 450°	30 - 45

INGREDIENT SUBSTITUTIONS

1 cup sifted **all-purpose flour** = 1 cup unsifted all-purpose flour minus 2 tbsp.
= 1¼ cups sifted cake and pastry flour
1 cup **sifted self-rising flour** = 1 cup sifted all-purpose flour plus 1½ tsp. baking powder and ½ tsp. salt
1 cup **granulated sugar** = 1 cup brown sugar, firmly packed
1 tbsp. **cornstarch** (for thickening) = 2 tbsp. flour
= 2 tsp. quick cooking tapioca
1 tsp. **baking powder** = ¼ tsp. baking soda plus ¾ tsp. cream of tartar
1 tsp. **double-acting baking powder** = 1½ tsp. phosphate baking powder or 2 tsp. tartrate baking powder
1 cup **butter** = 1 cup margarine (hard or brick-type)
= 1 cup shortening
1 cup **liquid honey** = 1¼ cups sugar plus ¼ cup liquid
1 cup **corn syrup** = 1 cup sugar plus ¼ cup liquid
1 cup **buttermilk** or **sour milk** = 1 tbsp. lemon juice or vinegar plus enough milk to make 1 cup (let stand 5 min.)
1 cup **buttermilk** = 1 cup plain yogurt
1 cup **sour cream** = 1 cup plain yogurt
1 cup **milk** = ½ cup evaporated milk plus ½ cup water
1 cup **skim milk** = 3 tbsp. skim milk powder plus 1 cup water
1 cup **cream** = ¾ cup milk plus ¼ cup butter
1 ounce **chocolate** (1 square) = 3 tbsp. cocoa plus 1 tbsp. butter or shortening
1 package **active dry yeast** = 1 tbsp. active dry yeast
1 **whole egg** = 2 egg yolks
1 cup **meat stock** = 1 cup consomme or 1 bouillon cube dissolved in 1 cup hot water
1 cup **tomato juice** = ½ cup tomato sauce plus ½ cup water
1 cup **tomato sauce** = ½ cup tomato paste plus ½ cup water
1 cup **tomato ketchup** = 1 cup tomato sauce plus ½ cup sugar plus 2 tbsp. vinegar
1 clove **garlic** = ⅛ tsp. garlic powder
1 tsp. **dry mustard** = 1 tbsp. prepared mustard
1 small **onion** = 1 tbsp. dehydrated, minced onion
1 tbsp. **fresh herbs** (eg) parsley, oregano = 1 tsp. dried
Juice of 1 **lemon** = 3 to 4 tbsp. bottled lemon juice

DESSERTS

ALY'S EASY DESSERT
Alyson Clifton

2 cans mandarin oranges, drained
1 can crushed pineapple, drained
1 pkg (250 g) cream cheese
1 L Cool Whip
Walnuts, chopped

Reserving a few orange segments and some walnuts, mash together oranges, pineapple and cream cheese. Stir in Cool Whip and walnuts. Refrigerate for 1 hour.

ORANGE CREAM FRUIT SALAD
Margaret Roller

20 oz can pineapple tidbits
16 oz can peach slices
11 oz can mandarin orange segments
3 medium bananas, sliced
2 medium apples, peeled, cored, cut into bite-sized pieces
3 3/4 oz pkg instant vanilla pudding mix (4 servings)
1 1/2 cups milk
3 oz frozen orange juice concentrate
3/4 cup sour cream

Drain canned fruits. In a large bowl combine fruits; set aside. In small bowl, combine dry pudding mix, milk, sour cream and orange juice concentrate. Beat with rotary beater until blended, 1 to 2 minutes. Fold into fruit mixture. Cover and chill.

FRUITY PHILLY FREEZE
Sandy Taylor

1 cup Christie Oreo baking crumbs
1/4 cup melted butter
2 (250 g) tubs Philadelphia light strawberry spreadable cream cheese
341 mL can frozen raspberry juice concentrate, thawed
1 L tub Cool Whip whipped topping, thawed

Mix Oreo baking crumbs with melted butter. Press into bottom of 9 inch square pan lined with foil. Beat cream cheese and slowly add juice concentrate, beating after each addition until smooth. Whisk in Cool Whip. Pour evenly over crust. Freeze until firm. Remove from freezer 15 minutes before serving. Makes 12 servings. For serving, sprinkle fresh strawberries, blueberries, or raspberries on top.

CREAM CHEESE DELIGHT
Carole Woodward

250 g pkg cream cheese
1 can mandarin oranges
10 oz can pineapple chunks

1 small carton whipping cream, whipped (or use small Dream Whip or single serving plain yogurt)

Drain cans of fruit and mix in bowl with cream cheese. Fold in the whipping cream. Chill and serve. Can be used as a dessert on its own or as a dip with fresh fruit platter.

ICELANDIC DELIGHT
Mary Krysko

1/2 lb Arrowroot cookies, crushed (1/2 box)
1 1/2 cups icing sugar
1/4 cup butter
2 eggs, well beaten

1/2 pt whip cream
1 can crushed pineapple, drained
1 Tbsp sugar
1 tsp vanilla

Put 1/2 cookie crumbs in greased 8x8 inch pan. In bowl, beat 2 eggs until creamy. Cream together icing sugar and butter and add beaten eggs. Spread on crumbs in pan. Whip cream very lightly and sweeten with sugar and vanilla. To whipped cream, add drained, crushed pineapple and spread over butter mixture. Cover with remaining crumbs and refrigerate. This freezes well, but thaw before serving. Also, doubles well.

ICE CREAM JELLO DESSERT
Ann Bishop

6 oz lime Jello
2 cups boiling water
1 jelly roll (3 small)

1 pt vanilla ice cream (2 cups)
Whipped cream for serving

Grease a round bowl. Slice jelly roll and line bowl. Make Jello, add ice cream. Pour slowly over jelly roll. Let set. Turn onto plate and decorate with whipped cream.

Mind unemployed is mind unenjoyed.

FRUIT SALAD WITH
COINTREAU CUSTARD SAUCE
Patricia McKinnon

1/3 cup lemon juice
1/4 cup orange marmalade
2 Tbsp sugar
1/4 cup Cointreau or orange
   liqueur
1 pineapple, cut in half
1 cantaloupe
1 honeydew melon
2 apples
4 oranges
1 pt strawberries
1/2 pt raspberries
1 pt blueberries

Bunch green grapes
Small bunch black grapes
2 kiwis
Cointreau Custard Sauce:
2/3 cup sugar
2 Tbsp cornstarch
2 cups milk
Grated peel of 1 orange
4 egg yolks
1 tsp vanilla
1/3 cup Cointreau/orange
   liqueur

Mix first 4 ingredients and pour over cut up fruit. Mix sauce ingredients in a double boiler until thickened. Pour sauce into pineapple halves and place fruit on top when serving.

CHERRY BERRIES ON A CLOUD
Jane Girard

6 large egg whites
1/4 tsp salt
2 cups whipping cream
1 tsp vanilla
1/2 tsp cream of tartar
2 3/4 cups sugar, divided

250 g pkg cream cheese,
   softened
2 cups miniature marshmallows
540 mL can cherry pie filling
1 tsp lemon juice
2 cups fresh strawberries,
   sliced

In a large bowl, beat egg whites, cream of tartar and salt until foamy. Beat in 1 3/4 cups of the sugar, one tablespoon at a time, and continue to beat until stiff and glossy. Do not under beat. Spread into buttered 9x13 inch baking pan. Bake at 275°F for one hour, then turn oven off and leave meringue in oven with door closed for 12 hours or longer. In a chilled bowl, beat whipping cream until stiff and add marshmallows.

In another bowl, beat together cream cheese, the remaining one cup sugar and vanilla. Gently fold whipped cream and marshmallows into cream cheese mixture. Spread over meringue. Cover and chill for 12 to 24 hours.

For topping, combine pie filling, lemon juice and strawberries in a bowl and mix. Place on top of meringue/cream cheese. Cut into pieces. Makes 12 servings.

CHANTILLY L'ORANGE

Cindy Walter

Meringue:
3 egg whites, at room
  temperature
1 1/4 cups icing sugar
Filling:
2 cups whipping cream
2 Tbsp Grand Marnier or
  orange liqueur
2 Tbsp finely grated orange
  peel

Chocolate Sauce:
4 (1 oz) squares semi-sweet
  chocolate
2 Tbsp margarine
2 Tbsp icing sugar
4 Tbsp water
1 Tbsp Grand Marnier
  (optional)

Meringue: Preheat oven to 275°F. Beat egg whites until very stiff. Sprinkle icing sugar over whites and fold in with a spatula. Spread into a foil-covered (I like parchment paper better) cookie sheet to one inch thickness and bake for one hour. Turn off oven and cool in open oven for at least one hour. Break into one-inch chunks.

Filling: Beat cream cheese until thick and add Grand Marnier and orange peel. Mix well. Fold in meringue pieces. Transfer to mold or pretty glass bowl. Cover and freeze.

Chocolate Sauce: Melt chocolate and margarine in microwave or double boiler. (Watch closely if using microwave, I reduce my power by half.) Do not boil! Add remaining ingredients and blend well. Add more water if sauce becomes too thick. Serve warm chocolate sauce over frozen chantilly in dessert bowls.

CHOCOLATE MOUSSE

Jacqueline Fassnacht

16 oz good-quality, dark
  chocolate in small pieces
1 1/2 Tbsp brandy
5 egg whites

4 egg yolks
1 1/4 cups whipping cream,
  whipped
3 Tbsp water

Place the chocolate, brandy and water in a heatproof bowl over a saucepan of hot water. Place over low heat and warm until chocolate has melted. Leave to cool for 5 minutes.

In a small clean dry bowl, beat egg whites until stiff peaks form. Add egg yolks to chocolate mixture one at a time, beating well after each addition. Fold cream into chocolate mixture and then fold in egg whites in two batches, using a large metal spoon. Pour chocolate mousse into serving bowls or glasses and refrigerate until set. Serves 8.

WHITE CHOCOLATE
PUMPKIN MOUSSE TART

Ann Bishop

40 gingersnap cookies (10 oz)
1/2 cup butter, melted
2 pkg unflavoured gelatin
1/4 cup dark rum or water
4 eggs
3/4 cup packed brown sugar
2 cups pumpkin puree
1 tsp cinnamon

1/2 tsp each ground ginger, nutmeg and salt
4 oz white chocolate, finely chopped
1/2 cup pasteurized egg whites
1/4 cup granulated sugar
1/2 cup whipping cream
1/2 cup whipping cream

In food processor, whirl gingersnap cookies to make 3 cups crumbs. Add butter; whirl until moistened. Press onto bottom and up sides of 9x1 1/2 inch round tart pan with removable bottom. Bake in centre of 350°F oven until firm to the touch, about 10 minutes. Let cool on rack.

Meanwhile in small bowl, sprinkle gelatin over rum (or water); set aside. In large bowl, beat eggs with brown sugar until pale; beat in pumpkin puree, cinnamon, ginger, nutmeg and salt. Transfer to saucepan. Cook over medium heat, stirring constantly, until candy thermometer registers 160°F, about 6 minutes. Remove from heat. Add gelatin mixture; stir until melted. Add white chocolate; stir until melted. Scrape into large bowl; refrigerate, stirring occasionally, until slightly colder than room temperature but not set, about 1 1/2 hours.

In bowl, beat egg whites until soft peaks form. Beat in granulated sugar 1 tablespoon at a time, until stiff glossy peaks form. In a separate bowl, whip cream; fold into pumpkin mixture. Fold in 1/3 of the egg whites, fold in remaining whites. Scrape into crust. Swirl decoratively. Refrigerate until set, about 4 hours. (Make ahead, cover loosely with plastic wrap and refrigerate for up to 2 days.)

In bowl, whip cream. Using piping bag fitted with 1/4 inch star tip, place tip at crust edge; pipe 1 inch swags, lifting tip at end swag, around edge. Garnish with white chocolate shards. Makes 8 to 12 servings.

*Happiness is not a station you arrive
at, but rather a manner of travelling*

MOCHA PRALINE CHOCOLATE TORTE   *Robin Burns*

6 egg whites
1/4 tsp salt
1/4 tsp cream of tartar
1 1/2 cups sugar
1/2 tsp almond extract
1/2 cup whole almonds

1/4 cup sugar
2 cups whipping cream
1 tsp instant coffee
1 Tbsp sugar
2 squares (2 oz/60 g)
    semi-sweet chocolate

Line 2 cookie sheets with parchment paper. Trace a 9 inch circle on the paper. In a large bowl, beat egg whites with salt and cream of tartar until soft peaks form. Continue beating and gradually add sugar. Add almond extract and beat until stiff peaks form. Spread mixture into circles, evening the tops. Bake at 275°F (140°C) for 1 hour. Turn oven off and leave meringues in oven overnight or reduce heat to 200°F (100°C) and bake for an additional one and a quarter hours. Remove and let cool. When cool, meringues may be frozen.

In a small heavy saucepan, cook almonds and sugar over medium-low heat, stirring until sugar melts and almonds start to crackle. When sugar is caramel coloured, pour mixture into buttered baking sheet or parchment paper. Let cool, and then crush with a mallet or in food processor. In a large bowl whip cream and coffee granules until thick. Beat in sugar. Fold in crushed praline (Coffee Crisp chocolate bars can be used to substitute for the praline if preferred.) Make chocolate shavings from squares of chocolate using a peeler.

To assemble, place one meringue on serving platter. Cover with half the cream filling and sprinkle with half the chocolate. Place second meringue on top and repeat the above. Refrigerate for at least 5 hours or overnight. Oetker Whipping Cream stabilizer can be used to "hold" the cream and keep it firm for cutting. Must make ahead. Serves 8 to 10.

*The secret of patience is doing
something else in the meantime.*

APPLE 'N CHEESE TORTE

Wendy Ternowesky

1/2 cup butter, softened
1/2 cup granulated sugar
1 cup all-purpose flour
1/2 cup raspberry or apricot
   jam
8 oz (250 g) pkg cream cheese,
   softened
1/4 cup granulated sugar

1 egg
1 tsp vanilla
3 cups apples, peeled and
   thinly sliced
1/3 cup granulated sugar
1/2 tsp cinnamon
1/2 cup sliced almonds

Cream butter and sugar together thoroughly. Blend in flour. Press evenly onto bottom and 1 1/2 inches up side of 8 1/2 inch springform pan. Spread jam evenly over bottom of crust. Beat all cream cheese, sugar, egg and vanilla together with electric mixer until smooth and light. Spread over jam. Toss apples, sugar and cinnamon together to coat well. Spoon over filling. Sprinkle with almonds. Bake at 450°F for 10 minutes, then reduce heat to 400°F for 25 to 30 minutes, or until set and apples are tender. Cool slightly then remove pan rim.

DEATH BY CHOCOLATE

Sandy Taylor

19 oz devil's food cake mix
   (baked and cooled according
   to pkg directions)
1/2 cup Kahlua
1 large tub Cool Whip

2 (4 serving size) instant
   chocolate pudding mix
4 cups milk
6 Skor bars, crushed

Mix pudding with milk, let sit. Tear cake into bite size pieces and divide into 2 bowls. Soak each with 1/4 cup Kahlua. Put 1/2 of cake in a very large glass bowl, cover with 1/2 of pudding, 1/2 Cool Whip and 1/2 of Skor bars. Repeat layers. Refrigerate overnight or at least 2 hours.

If you haven't any wrinkles,
you haven't laughed enough.

CHOCOLATE CHEESECAKE

2 oz butter
2 oz icing sugar
6 oz plain digestive biscuits
8 oz cream cheese, softened

2 oz brown sugar, soft
2 Tbsp chocolate spread
2 cartons chocolate flavoured
   yogurt

Melt the butter in a saucepan and stir in the crushed biscuits. Press evenly into the base of a loose bottomed round cake tin. Chill. Whip the cream and icing sugar stiffly. In a separate bowl, cream the soft cream cheese and brown sugar, beat in the yogurt and chocolate spread, then add the whipped cream. Pour over biscuit base and chill for 3 to 4 hours until firm. Grate the plain chocolate coarsely. Decorate the top of the cheesecake with plain chocolate, whipped cream, if desired, and chocolate flakes.

WARM DATE PUDDING
WITH BUTTERSCOTCH SAUCE   *Jo-Ann Martin*

1 1/4 cups chopped dates
1 tsp baking soda
5 Tbsp butter
3/4 cup sugar
2 eggs

1 cup flour
1 cup brown sugar, firmly
   packed
1 cup cream
1 cup butter

Grease deep 20 cm round cake pan. Line base with paper and grease paper. Combine dates and water in pan, bring to boil. Remove from heat, add soda, stand for 5 minutes. Blend or process until smooth.

Cream butter and sugar in small bowl with electric mixer until well combined. Beat in eggs 1 at a time. Gently fold in sifted flour, then date mixture. Pour mixture into prepared pan, bake in moderate oven about 55 minutes or until cooked through. Cover pudding with foil if it becomes too dark during cooking. Stand pudding 10 minutes before turning onto wire rack over oven tray. Pour 1/4 cup sauce over pudding, return to moderate oven, bake uncovered, further 5 minutes. Serve pudding with remaining sauce.

To make butterscotch sauce, combine flour, brown sugar, cream and butter in pan, stir over heat, without boiling until sugar is dissolved, then simmer, stirring for 3 minutes.

WARM BLUEBERRY
TOPPING FOR ICE CREAM
Vi Sakaki

2 tsp unsalted butter   **1/4 cup sugar**
1 pt blueberries

Melt butter over medium heat. When melted, add blueberries and sugar. Cook, stirring until blueberries release juices, about 2 minutes. Cool slightly, spoon over ice cream. Garnish with more blueberries. Can be refrigerated and used cold as well.

CAKES

RAW APPLE CAKE
Ella Klann

4 cups unpeeled, diced apples   **2 tsp cinnamon**
2 cups dark brown raw sugar   **2 tsp soda**
1/2 cup vegetable oil   **2 cups flour**
1 cup walnuts, chopped   **2 eggs**

Mix apples and sugar together, add oil and mix again. Add dry ingredients. Lastly add well beaten eggs. Bake in a 9x13 inch or springform greased pan for 1 hour at 350°F.

CARROT CAKE
Cathy Guarasci

1 1/2 cups flour   **8 oz can crushed pineapple,**
1 1/4 cups sugar   **drained**
1 1/2 tsp baking soda   **2/3 cup coconut**
1 1/2 tsp cinnamon   **1/2 cup chopped walnuts**
1/4 tsp salt   **1 small pkg light cream cheese**
1 1/4 cups cooked carrots,   **2 Tbsp butter or margarine (or**
mashed   **use a little milk instead)**
2/3 cup oil   **1 tsp vanilla or rum flavoring**
2 eggs, slightly beaten   **1 1/2 cups icing sugar (or more**
1/2 tsp vanilla   **for desired consistency)**

In 9 inch pan, mix first 6 ingredients. Add next 3 and mix. Add last 3 and mix. Bake at 350°F for 40 to 50 minutes. Cool cake and then ice. Beat icing ingredients, cheese, margarine, vanilla, and icing sugar together and spread over cake. This cake freezes well.

CHOCOLATE CARROT/ZUCCHINI CAKE   *Margot Hollaway*

1 3/4 cups sugar
1/2 cup oil
1/4 cup butter
2 eggs
1 tsp vanilla
1/2 cup buttermilk
2 1/2 cups flour
4 Tbsp cocoa

1/2 tsp cinnamon
1/2 tsp cloves
1 tsp baking soda
1/2 tsp baking powder
1 cup grated carrot
1 cup grated zucchini
1/2 cup chocolate chips

Cream sugar, oil, butter, eggs, vanilla and buttermilk together. Sift dry ingredients and add to above. Stir in carrot, zucchini and chips. Bake in greased 9x13 inch pan, or bundt pan at 325°F for 60 minutes.

TROPICAL CARROT CAKE   *Patricia McKinnon*

2 cups flour
2 tsp baking powder
1 tsp each soda, salt, nutmeg,
   allspice and cinnamon
4 eggs
2 cups sugar (or less)
3/4 cup vegetable oil
2 cups shredded carrots
8 oz can crushed pineapple,
   drained (3/4 cup)

1 cup walnuts, chopped
1/2 cup coconut (optional) or
   raisins
6 oz cream cheese
2 cups icing sugar
2 Tbsp orange or lemon juice
1 tsp vanilla
1 tsp grated orange or lemon
   peel

For cake, mix all ingredients thoroughly. Place in greased 9x13 inch pan and bake at 350°F for approximately 30 to 35 minutes. When cake is cool, mix cheese, icing sugar, juice, vanilla and peel to make frosting and ice cake.

*Gossip is the art of saying nothing
in a way that leaves nothing unsaid.*

DARK CHOCOLATE CAKE
Jackie Pawson

18 oz pkg dark devil's food
  cake mix
3 3/4 oz pkg instant chocolate
  pudding mix
1 cup sour cream or yogurt

1/2 cup cooking oil
1/2 cup warm water
4 eggs, beaten
1 1/2 cups semi-sweet
  chocolate chips

In large bowl, combine all ingredients except chocolate chips. Beat for 4 minutes. Fold in chips. Bake in greased and floured 12 cup bundt pan at 350°F for 50 to 60 minutes or until toothpick comes out clean. Cool in pan for 15 minutes then turn out onto serving plate. Dust with icing sugar.

DEVIL'S FOOD CAKE COCKAIGNE
Olga Langevin

2 (4 oz) chocolate
1/2 cup milk
1 cup brown sugar
1 egg yolk
2 cups cake flour
1 tsp soda
1/2 tsp salt
1 cup white sugar
1/2 cup softened butter

1/4 cup water
1/2 cup milk
1 tsp vanilla
2 egg whites
2 cups brown sugar
1 cup cream (or 1/2 cup milk
  plus 1/2 cup butter)
3 Tbsp butter
1 tsp vanilla

Combine chocolate, milk, brown sugar and egg yolk in the top of a double boiler. Cook and stir over, not in, hot water. Remove from heat when thickened. Set aside. Sift together dry ingredients. Beat in 2 egg yolks one at a time. Add water, milk, vanilla and egg whites to the flour and butter mixture. Stir in chocolate custard mixture and stir until smooth. Whip 2 egg whites, fold them lightly into cake mixture. Preheat oven to 350°F. Bake in 2 greased 9 inch layer pans for approximately 25 minutes. Cool in pans, turn out onto serving plate. When cooled, spread with Caramel Icing.

To make icing, mix brown sugar and cream in a small saucepan. Cover and cook for 3 minutes. Uncover and cook without stirring to 238 to 240°F. Add 3 tablespoons butter. Add vanilla. Beat the icing until it is thick and creamy. Add some cream if too thick. Pour icing over cake. Can garnish icing with chocolate.

MOCHA CAKE
Cathy Guarasci

36 single graham wafers
1 pt whipping cream
3 Tbsp chocolate sauce

3/4 cup icing sugar
2 tsp instant coffee
1 tsp vanilla

Place a layer of 9 wafers in 8x8 inch pan. Whip cream until almost stiff, then add other ingredients while still whipping. Cover the layer of wafers with 1/4 of the whipping cream mixture. Continue layering until all wafers are used and cream mixture is on the top. Cover with plastic wrap and refrigerate for at least 24 hours. When ready to serve, top with grated chocolate or toasted almonds.

OATMEAL RAISIN CAKE
Joyce Parlin

1 cup oatmeal (not instant)
1 1/2 cups hot water
3/4 cup brown sugar
3/4 cup white sugar
1/2 cup margarine
2 eggs
1 1/2 cups raisins
1 tsp baking soda

2 tsp cinnamon
1 1/2 cups white flour
1/2 cup vegetable oil
3/4 cup brown sugar
6 tsp cream or milk
1 tsp vanilla
1 1/2 cups fine shredded
  coconut

Soak oatmeal in hot water until absorbed. Cream sugars, margarine and eggs together. Add oatmeal, stir. Add raisins, stir. Add flour, cinnamon and soda and stir. Bake in 9x13 inch pan in oven at 350°F for 30 minutes. Prepare broiled topping while cake is baking by mixing flour, oil, brown sugar, cream, vanilla and coconut well. Spoon on top of cake as soon as it comes out of the oven and spread gently. Broil for about 3 to 4 minutes, until bubbly.

Better to remain silent and be thought a
fool than to speak out and remove all doubt.

ARMENIAN ORANGE CAKE
Kathryn Waldie

2 cups brown sugar
2 cups all purpose flour, sifted
1/2 cup butter
1/2 tsp salt
2 Tbsp fresh orange peel,
   grated

1/2 tsp allspice
1 tsp baking soda
1 cup dairy sour cream
1 egg, slightly beaten
1/2 cup chopped nuts (walnuts,
   cashews, almonds)

Combine brown sugar, flour, butter, salt, orange peel and allspice in a medium sized bowl. Blend with a pastry blender or a fork, until mixture is crumbly and completely blended. Grease a 9 inch square pan. (A springform pan is a good idea if serving at the table.) Spoon in half the crumb mixture. Stir soda into sour cream and mix into the remaining crumbs, adding the egg. Pour batter over crumbs and sprinkle with chopped nuts. Bake in 350°F oven for 40 to 45 minutes. Serve warm topped with orange whipped cream.

PUMPKIN CAKE
Donna Tratch

3 eggs, slightly beaten
1 large can pumpkin
1 1/2 cups white sugar
1 tsp salt
1 tsp ginger
2 tsp cinnamon

1/2 tsp cloves
3 cups evaporated milk
1 pkg yellow cake mix
1 cup margarine, melted
1 cup chopped nuts

Grease a 10x15 inch pan. Beat eggs, add pumpkin, spices, sugar and milk. Pour into pan. Sprinkle one package yellow cake mix overtop of the mixture. Drizzle 1 cup melted margarine over top. Sprinkle with 1 cup chopped nuts (pecans are nice). Bake at 350°F for 1 1/4 hours or until done. Test with a toothpick.

PLUM CAKE
Jacqueline Fassnacht

1 cup sugar
1 lb butter
4 1/4 cups flour

4 eggs
30 fresh black Italian plums

Beat sugar and butter. Add eggs one at a time, beat well. Add flour and mix. Pat into cookie sheet. Place plums on top, sliced or 1/2s (skin up). Bake until brown in 350°F oven for approximately 1 hour. Serve with whipping cream.

PUMPKIN CHOCOLATE CAKE
Lorraine Giordano

3 cups flour
2 cups sugar
1 tsp salt
1 tsp cinnamon
2 tsp baking powder
2 tsp baking soda
1 cup cooking oil

4 eggs, unbeaten
2 cups canned or fresh
    pumpkin, cooked and mashed
1 cup chopped nuts
3/4 cup chocolate chips

Stir dry ingredients together. Add remaining ingredients in order. Mix well. Bake in greased 10 inch square pan at 375°F for 1 hour. Serve plain or with whipping cream.

RAISIN AND RUM CAKE
Gretchen Hopkins

1 1/2 cups raisins
2 Tbsp rum
1 cup butter, softened
2 cups sugar
4 eggs
3 cups all purpose flour
2 tsp baking powder

1/4 tsp salt
1 cup sour cream
1 Tbsp grated orange rind
3/4 cup sugar
1/3 cup rum
1/4 cup orange juice

Combine raisins and rum; cover and set aside for 2 hours. Combine butter, sugar and eggs; beat with electric mixer until light and fluffy. Combine flour, baking powder and salt; stir into butter mixture alternately with sour cream. Stir in orange rind and raisins. Pour batter into greased and floured 12-cup bundt pan. Bake in 350°F oven for 1 1/4 hours or until toothpick inserted in center comes out clean. Cool 10 minutes. Remove from pan to wire rack.

To make glaze mix sugar, rum, and orange juice. Stir until well combined. Brush hot cake with Rum Glaze; cool.

*Fortune does not change
people; it only unmasks them.*

CHOCOLATE YULE LOG

Donna Wisniowski

6 egg whites (should be room
   temperature)
3/4 cup sugar
6 egg yolks
1/3 cup unsweetened cocoa
1 1/2 tsp vanilla extract
Dash salt

Confectioners' sugar
1 1/2 cups heavy cream, chilled
1/2 cup confectioners' sugar
1/4 cup unsweetened cocoa
2 tsp instant coffee
1 tsp vanilla extract
Candied cherries

Line bottom of a greased cookie sheet with wax paper. Preheat oven to 375°F. Beat egg whites until soft peaks forms. Add 1/2 cup sugar to egg whites 2 tablespoons at a time until stiff peaks are formed.

In a separate bowl mix egg yolk, add 1/2 cup sugar 2 tablespoons at a time until mixture is thick. In another bowl, mix at low speed cocoa, vanilla and salt just until smooth. Fold cocoa mixture and egg yolk mixture into egg whites just until blended. Spread evenly in pan and bake for 15 minutes until surface springs back. Sift confectioners' sugar in a 10x15 inch rectangle on a clean linen towel. Turn cake out onto sugar, roll up and cool on rack seam side down.

Make filling by mixing together heavy cream, confectioners' sugar, cocoa, coffee and vanilla. Unroll cake, spread with filling and reroll. Decorate with confectioners' sugar and candied cherries.

CHRISTMAS LOG

Maureen Cockburn

6 egg whites
1/2 cup white sugar
4 Tbsp cocoa
4 Tbsp flour, sifted
1/4 tsp salt

6 egg whites
1/2 tsp cream of tartar
1/2 cup white sugar
Whipped cream

Beat egg yolks until thick and lemon colored. Gradually beat in 1/2 cup sugar. Add sifted flour, cocoa and salt. Blend well. Beat egg whites. Spread 1/2 inch thick in shallow pan 10x15 inch that has been lined with well greased paper. Bake at 325°F for 20 to 25 minutes. Turn upside down on a towel sprinkled with icing sugar. Remove paper and roll up with towel to prevent sticking. When cool, unroll and spread with whipped cream, sugar and vanilla. Roll up carefully. Frost side and top with chocolate butter icing. Pull spatula down the roll to simulate back of log. Decorate with sprays of holly. Use maraschino cherries for red coloring and green gum drops or cherries for leaves.

TEQUILA CAKE

Frank Sakaki

1 cup water
1 tsp baking soda
1 cup sugar
1 tsp salt
1 cup brown sugar

1 Tbsp lemon juice
4 large eggs
Nuts
1 bottle tequila
2 cups dried fruit

Sample the tequila to check the quality. To be sure it is of the highest quality, pour one level cup and drink. Repeat. Turn on the electric mixer. Beat one cup of butter in a large fluffy bowl. Add one teaspoon of sugar. Beat again.

At this point it's best to make sure the tequila is still okay. Try another cup, just in case. Turn off the mixerer thingy. Break 2 leggs and add to the bowl and chuck in the cup of dried fruit. Pick the dang fruit up off floor. Mix on the turner. If the fried druit gets stuck in the beaterers just pry it loose with a drewscriver. Sample the tequila to check for tonsistikity. Nex, sift two cups of salt. Or something. Check the tequila. Now shift the lemon juice and add one table. Add a spoon of sugar, or somefink. Whatever you can find. Greash the oven. Turn the cake tin 360 degrees and try not to fall over. Finally, throw the bowl through the window. Finish the tequila and wipe counter with the cat. And then start drinking plenty of water.

COOKIES

RUM/BOURBON BALLS

Audrey Karpoff

3 cups (750 mL) vanilla wafers,
  crushed
1 cup ground pecans
1 cup confectioners' sugar
3 Tbsp light corn syrup

1 1/2 Tbsp cocoa powder
1/2 cup bourbon or rum
1/2 cup confectioners' sugar (to
  roll cookies in)

Mix all ingredients together. Form into balls. Roll each ball in confectioners' sugar. Makes 36.

Education is not received; it is achieved.

ALMOND DIAMONDS

Alyson Clifton

1 cup unsalted butter, softened
1 cup sugar
2 large eggs
1/2 tsp salt
1 tsp vanilla extract
1/2 tsp almond extract
3 cups flour

White from 1 large egg, beaten
with a fork
1 1/2 cups sliced natural
almonds
1/4 cup coarse (crystal) white
sugar

In a large bowl with mixer on medium speed, beat all ingredients except flour until fluffy. On low speed, add flour and beat just until blended. Divide dough in half, wrap separately and refrigerate for 1 hour, until firm.

Heat oven to 325°F. Have cookie sheet(s) ready. On lightly floured waxed paper with a floured rolling pin, roll half the dough into a 12 inch square. Slide onto a cookie sheet and freeze for 10 minutes. Cut dough crosswise in 8 strips, then diagonally in 8 strips, forming diamonds with triangles around edges. Lift with a flexible metal spatula and place 1 inch apart on ungreased cookie sheet(s). Repeat with remaining dough.

Brush dough with egg white, gently press almonds into dough, then brush almonds with egg white and sprinkle with coarse sugar. Bake for 8 to 10 minutes until edges are lightly browned. Remove to wire racks to cool. Store in airtight container at cool room temperature up to 1 week or freeze up to 3 months.

COWBOY COOKIES

Lois Wilson

1 cup Crisco shortening
1 cup sugar
1 cup brown sugar
2 eggs
1 tsp vanilla
2 cups flour
1 1/2 tsp baking powder

1 tsp baking soda
1/2 tsp salt
2 cups regular rolled Quaker
oats
1 cup chocolate chips
1/2 cup walnuts or pecans,
chopped (optional)

In a large mixing bowl, cream together, shortening, sugar and brown sugar. Add eggs and vanilla and mix well. Add 1 cup of flour, baking powder, soda and salt and mix thoroughly. Add 1 more cup of flour and blend together. Add rolled oats, chocolate chips, nuts and stir. Drop by spoonful on an ungreased cookie sheet. Bake for 12 minutes at 350°F. Best if not overdone. Makes 3 dozen.

ORANGE-CHOCOLATE BISCOTTI
Alyson Clifton

1/4 cup butter, softened
1 1/4 cups sugar, divided
1 Tbsp finely grated orange
  peel
1 tsp baking powder
4 large eggs

2 cups flour
2/3 cup semi-sweet chocolate
  mini chips
2/3 cup shelled lightly salted
  pistachio nuts

Heat oven to 350°F. Lightly grease a large cookie sheet. In a large bowl with mixer on high speed, beat butter, 1 cup sugar, the peel and baking powder until well blended. Beat in 3 eggs. On low speed, beat in flour just until blended. Stir in chips and nuts.

Turn dough out on a well-floured work surface (dough is sticky). Divide dough in quarters. Roll each portion into a 9 inch log. Place logs 3 inches apart on prepared baking sheet. Beat remaining egg in a small bowl with a fork. Brush on logs, then sprinkle with the remaining 1/4 cup sugar.

Bake for 20 to 25 minutes until golden brown. Let cool on sheet on a wire rack for 5 minutes. Loosen with a spatula and remove to a cutting board. Wipe cookie sheet with a paper towel. With a long, sharp knife, cut each log diagonally in 1/2 inch thick slices. Arrange slices upright on cookie sheet. Bake for 15 to 17 minutes longer until crisp. Remove to wire rack to cool (cookies will get even more crisp). Store in airtight container at room temperature up to 3 weeks or freeze up to 3 months.

DANISH KLEINER
Inger-Lise Koetke

3 eggs
1 cup sugar
1/2 tsp salt
4 Tbsp cream
1/2 cup butter
1 tsp baking powder

3 to 4 cups flour
1 tsp vanilla or cardamom
1 tsp lemon rind
1 1/2 lb Crisco shortening for
  frying
Icing sugar

Beat eggs, sugar and salt. Add cream and melted butter. Sift flour with baking powder, and add enough to make batter stiff enough to roll out like cookies. Cut into diamond shape, make slit in center and pull one end through slit. Cook in deep fat until light brown. Best to cook only 4 to 6 at a time. Turn with kitchen fork and place on brown paper to cool. When cooled, cover with sifted icing sugar.

DUTCH COOKIES
Vi Sakaki

2 cups all purpose flour
1 tsp ground cinnamon
1/2 tsp salt
1 cup unsalted butter, softened

1 cup sugar
1 large egg, separated
1 cup chopped pecans (about
  1/2 lb)

Put oven rack in middle and preheat oven to 325°F. Butter pan. Whisk together flour, cinnamon and salt. Beat together butter and sugar with electric mixer at medium-high speed until pale and fluffy. Beat in yolk. Reduce speed to low, then mix in flour mixture until it is combined. Spread batter evenly in 15x10x1 inch pan with offset spatula. Lightly beat egg white, then brush some of it over batter and sprinkle evenly with pecans. Bake until top is golden brown and edges begin to pull away from sides of the pan, about 35 to 40 minutes. Cool in pan on rack for 10 minutes. Cut while still warm into 2 inch squares or halve squares diagonally into triangles and cool completely on rack.

SLEEPY HOUSE
CHOCOLATE GINGER COOKIES
Yvonne Manville

3 cups brown sugar
2 cups butter or margarine
2 eggs
2 tsp vanilla
4 cups all purpose flour
2 tsp baking soda

1 Tbsp each cinnamon and
  ginger
1 tsp salt
2 cups pecans, chopped
2 cups chocolate chips

Cream together the sugar and butter or margarine. Add the eggs, one at a time, then the vanilla extract. Sift together all the dry ingredients and add the nuts and chocolate chips. Mix well. Put in a Ziploc bag to keep in fridge for at least an hour. Spoon 1 heaped teaspoon each, onto slightly greased cookie sheet. Press down with the tines of a fork. Bake at 375°F for 10 to 15 minutes. Allow to cool for 10 minutes before lifting. Stores well in cookie tin.

Do you spend more than you make on things you don't need to impress people you don't like?

SEVEN LAYER COOKIES

Cathy Guarasci

1/4 lb stick butter
2 cups graham wafer crumbs
6 oz pkg chocolate chips
6 oz pkg butterscotch chips

1 cup coconut
Roasted mixed and salted nuts
1 can Eagle Brand

Melt butter and pour into 9x13 inch pan. Spread evenly. Top with next ingredients, one layer at a time. Nuts can be as many or few as you like. Pour Eagle Brand over top as evenly as possible. Bake at 350°F for 25 to 30 minutes. Cut when cool.

SNICKERDOODLES

Lois Wilson

1 cup shortening or butter
1 1/2 cups sugar
2 eggs
2 3/4 cups sifted flour

2 tsp cream of tartar
1 tsp baking soda
1/4 tsp sugar
2 tsp cinnamon

Preheat oven to 400°F. Mix shortening, sugar and eggs thoroughly. Blend flour, cream of tartar, baking soda and salt. Stir into shortening mixture. Shape dough into 1 inch balls. Roll balls in mixture of sugar and cinnamon. Place 2 inches apart on ungreased baking sheet and bake for 8 to 10 minutes.

SHORTBREAD

Ann Bishop

1 lb butter, softened
1 cup berry sugar

4 cups all purpose flour

Cream butter and sugar well. Add flour slowly, working it with your hands mixing it well. Roll out to 1/2 inch thickness. Cut as desired.

Dust cookie sheets lightly with flour. Put cookies on pans and bake at 325°F until lightly golden, approximately 15 minutes.

Everybody is ignorant - but only on different subjects.

GINNY'S SHORTBREAD

Ginge

1 cup soft butter
1/2 cup icing sugar

1 1/2 cups all purpose flour

Beat the butter until fluffy. Slowly add the icing sugar and beat until fluffy. Add flour slowly and beat. Drop by small spoonfuls onto ungreased cookie sheet. Bake at 300°F for 30 minutes, checking regularly as they burn easily.

MOM'S SCOTCH SHORTBREAD

Wendy Ternowesky

1 cup rice flour
1 cup fine sugar

3 cups all purpose flour
1 lb butter, softened

Cream together, butter, sugar, and rice flour. Gradually add flour. Mix well for about 15 minutes. Roll it out in 11x16 inch baking sheet with rolling pin. Prick it up and down with a fork. Bake at 300°F for 1 hour. Watch it closely. Immediately cut into squares 12 on the long side and 18 on the short side.

SCOTCH COOKIES

Kay MacCormack

1 lb butter, softened
4 cups white flour

1 cup brown sugar, packed

Mix well in a large bowl. Roll dough and cut in desired shapes. Place on cookie sheets and bake in oven at 300°F for 10 to 15 minutes.

CHRISTMAS TREATS

Trish Markwick

Graham wafers
Flaked almonds
1/2 lb melted butter

3/4 cup brown sugar
1 Tbsp corn syrup

Line a 9x13 inch pan with graham wafers. Generously spread flaked almonds over wafers. Melt butter, add brown sugar and corn syrup. Heat to a rolling boil, until temperature rises to 215°F. Pour mixture immediately over wafers and almonds. Spread evenly and bake for 8 minutes at 350°F. Cool and break up into bite-sized pieces.

PEPPERMINT STICKS

Alyson Clifton

1 cup unsalted butter, at room
  temperature
1 cup sugar
1/2 tsp vanilla extract
2 large eggs
2 3/4 cups flour
1/4 tsp salt
2 tsp mint extract

12 drops each green and red
  food colour
1 1/2 cups confectioners' sugar
1 1/2 Tbsp water
  (approximately)
12 each green and red
  peppermint candies, crushed

In a large bowl with mixer on medium speed, beat the butter, sugar and vanilla until fluffy. Beat in eggs, one at a time. On low speed, gradually add the flour and salt; beat just until blended. Divide dough in half. Shape one half into a 6 inch disk; wrap and refrigerate. Stir the mint extract into other half and divide that half in half. Stir green food colour into one half, red into the other (colours will be pale). Shape each into 5 inch disk; wrap and refrigerate 1 hour, until firm.

Heat oven to 350°F. Have cookie sheets ready. Cut uncolored dough in 12 equal wedges. Cut each disk tinted dough into 6 equal wedges. On a light floured surface, roll 1 plain wedge and 1 tinted wedge into 15 inch long ropes (keep rest of dough refrigerated). Place side by side. Cut crosswise in quarters. Holding end of a plain and tinted strand, twist together from one end to the other (handle gently, dough is soft). Place 1 inch apart on ungreased cookie sheet(s). Repeat with remaining dough. Bake for 11 to 13 minutes.

SQUARES

STICKY SQUARES

Audrey Davies

60 medium marshmallows
1/4 cup margarine or butter
5 cups corn flakes

2 cups flaked almonds
2 cups long coconut
1 tsp vanilla

Melt butter or margarine in microwave in a large microwave bowl. Add marshmallows, stir to mix. Heat until melted. Add vanilla to melted marshmallows. Add remaining ingredients and press lightly in a greased 9x13 inch pan. Cut into squares or bars.

BROWNIE RECIPE
"THE BEST ONE EVER"
Patricia Markwick

2 cups brown sugar
1 cup butter or margarine
4 eggs
2 tsp vanilla
1 cup flour
1/2 cup cocoa (Fry's is best)
1/2 cup chopped nuts
   (optional)

1/2 cup butter or margarine
5 Tbsp cocoa
1/8 tsp salt
2 tsp vanilla
2 cups icing sugar
3 to 4 Tbsp hot water

Cream brown sugar with butter or margarine. Add eggs one at a time and then add vanilla. Combine flour, cocoa and nuts together and then add to the moistened ingredients. Place in a 9x12 inch pan and bake for 30 minutes at 300°F. In glass bowl, microwave butter, cocoa, salt and vanilla for 1 minute. Add icing sugar. Beat well with mixer. While beating add 3 to 4 tablespoons hot water. Beat until smooth. Spread icing over well cooled brownie mixture.

SURREY'S BEST DATE SQUARES
Paula Fenby

1 cup pitted dates
1 cup water
1/2 cup brown sugar
1 tsp lemon juice (or more to
   taste)
1/2 tsp ground cardamom
1/2 tsp cinnamon
1 cup brown sugar

1 1/4 cups rolled oats
1 1/2 cups all-purpose flour
1/4 cup wheat germ
1/2 tsp salt
1/2 tsp ground cardamom
1/2 tsp cinnamon
3/4 cup butter

For filling, measure dates, water, brown sugar, lemon juice, ground cardamom and cinnamon into saucepan. Simmer gently until smooth and thick. Measure sugar, oats, flour, wheat germ, salt, and spices into mixing bowl. Rub in butter until mixture is crumbly. Spread half crumb mixture in 9x9 inch pan; press down. Spread with date filling. Add remaining crumb mixture; press flat with spoon. Bake in hot oven, 400°F for 20 to 25 minutes. Cut when cool.

No knowledge, no doubt.

CLASSIC LEMON BARS
Vi Sakaki

Base:
1/4 cup butter or margarine, softened
1/4 cup sugar
1 cup flour
Pinch salt
Topping:
1 cup sugar

2 Tbsp flour
1/4 tsp baking powder
Pinch salt
1 large egg
1 large egg white
Grated zest of 1 large lemon
3 Tbsp lemon juice
Icing sugar for sprinkling

Preheat oven to 350°F. In a medium bowl, beat butter and sugar until creamy. Add flour and salt and stir until well combined and crumbly. Press into the bottom of an 8x8 inch pan that has been greased or sprayed with nonstick spray. Bake for about 12 minutes, until just barely starting to turn golden around the edges.

Using the same bowl, combine sugar, flour, baking powder and salt. Add egg, egg white, lemon zest and juice and stir until smooth. Pour over the base. Return to the oven for 25 to 30 minutes, until golden and bubbly around the edges. Cool completely in the pan on a wire rack before cutting. Sprinkle cooled bars with icing sugar.

CINNAMON STREUSEL
Jacqueline Fassnacht

3/4 cup warm water
1 tsp sugar
1 pkg yeast
1/4 cup sugar
1 tsp salt
2 1/4 cups flour, divided
1 egg

1/4 cup butter
30 fresh black Italian plums
2 Tbsp butter
1/3 cup white or brown sugar
2 Tbsp flour
2 tsp cinnamon
1/2 cup chopped nuts

Mix warm water, sugar and yeast in a bowl. When dissolved, add sugar, salt and 1 cup of flour. Beat well for 2 minutes. Add egg, butter and beat to blend well. Beat in another 1 1/4 cups flour, beating until smooth. Drop small spoonfuls of dough onto cookie sheet. Top with halved plums, pour a little cream overtop (whipping cream can be used but just a drizzle on top, as too much will make dough become soggy). Mix topping ingredients together and sprinkle on top of streusel. Let rise for 45 to 60 minutes. Bake at 350°F for approximately 1 hour.

RIBBON FINGER JELLO
Dorothy Cunningham

4 (3 oz pkg) Jello (orange, lemon, lime and strawberry)
6 envelopes Knox gelatin

1 can Eagle Brand condensed milk
4 3/4 cups boiling water
1/4 cup water

Dissolve 2 envelopes gelatin in 1/4 cup water. Add 3/4 cup boiling water. Stir until gelatin is dissolved. Combine with condensed milk, divide in 3 parts and cool.

Mix each box of Jello with an envelope of gelatin. Add 1 cup boiling water to each Jello mixture, stir constantly until Jello dissolves.

Pour 1 Jello into a 9x13 inch (Pam sprayed) pan, and refrigerate for 20 minutes. Pour 1 part of milk mixture on top, and refrigerator for 15 minutes. Pour another layer of Jello; alternate with milk, refrigerate 15 minutes between each layer, ending with Jello (lime, milk, orange, milk, lemon, milk, strawberry). After the second layer of milk, heat the third portion of milk slightly, so it isn't too solid to pour. Make sure the first layer of Jello is well set, before continuing. Cut in diamond shaped pieces to serve.

PIES

BANOFEE PIE

7 oz digestive biscuits
3 oz butter
14 oz tin condensed milk
3 large ripe bananas

1 medium carton whipping cream
1 small tin mandarin oranges
1/2 cup crushed chocolate flakes

Heat oven to 375°F. Crush biscuits, melt butter and mix. Press into round push-up bottom type cheesecake tin. Bake in oven for 10 minutes. Boil tin of milk for 1 3/4 hours, check water level regularly and turn tin in saucepan every half hour. Cut up bananas and arrange on top of biscuit base. When opening tin of boiled milk beware! Very hot and liable to spurt out. Mixture will be thick but spread on top of bananas. When cold spread beaten cream on top of caramel mixture and arrange fruit around edge. Scatter crushed flakes on top of pie. The mandarin oranges help to reduce the over-sweet taste of toffee mixture.

FRUIT FLAN
Pat Johnston

1/2 cup butter
1/3 cup sugar
1 cup flour
2 pears (Bartlett, Bosc)
1 apple
4 oz cream cheese
1/2 cup sugar

2 eggs
3/4 cup milk (or use cream and
  milk)
1/2 tsp vanilla
1/2 tsp cinnamon
1/4 cup sliced almonds

Cream butter and sugar until light. Beat 3 to 5 minutes. Gently beat in flour. Pat into bottom and up sides (one inch or more) of 8 inch springform pan. Beat cream cheese, add sugar. Add eggs one at a time, beating smooth. Add milk and vanilla and set aside. Peel, halve and core fruit. Slice thin. Place in crust, piling slightly higher in centre. Pour filling over fruit. Sprinkle with almonds and cinnamon. Bake at 425°F for 10 minutes and 350°F for 45 minutes or until custard is set in the centre. Serve at room temperature.

MOIST COCONUT PIE
Sandy Taylor

4 eggs
1/4 cup butter, softened
1/2 cup flour
1/2 cup milk

1 cup icing sugar
1 cup coconut
400 mL can coconut milk

Blend or process all ingredients until smooth. Pour into greased 9 inch pie plate. Bake in 350°F oven for 1 hour. Cool to room temperature, turn onto serving plate. Can be made a day before. To serve decorate with whipped cream, cherries and toasted shredded coconut.

SUMMER PIE
Alyson Clifton

250 g pkg cream cheese
1/4 cup icing sugar
2 Tbsp sour cream
1 tsp vanilla
1 ready made crumb crust
2 kiwi fruit, peeled, thinly sliced

3 cups medium whole
  strawberries
1 pkg fruit glaze
1/2 cup whipping cream,
  whipped

Beat together first 4 ingredients, until smooth. Pour into crumb crust and chill for 3 to 4 hours. Arrange fruit over cheese mixture. Prepare fruit glaze as per package instructions and pour over fruit. Serve with whipping cream.

PUMPKIN FLUFF PIE
Maureen Cockburn

3/4 cup brown sugar
1 envelope unflavored gelatin
1/2 tsp salt
1 tsp cinnamon
1/2 tsp nutmeg
1/4 tsp ginger
3 slightly beaten egg yolks
3/4 cup milk
1 1/4 cups canned or mashed
   cooked pumpkin

3 egg whites
1/3 cup granulated sugar
Corn Flake Crust:
1 cup packaged corn flake
   crumbs or 4 cups corn
   flakes, coarsely crushed
2 Tbsp sugar
2 Tbsp finely chopped walnuts
1/3 cup butter or margarine,
   melted

Mix together all ingredients of the corn flake crust. Press firmly in 9 inch pie plate. Bake in 375°F oven for about 8 minutes or until edges are lightly browned. Cool.

In saucepan, combine brown sugar, gelatin, salt and spices. Combine egg yolks and milk; stir into brown sugar mixture. Cook and stir until mixture comes to a boil. Remove from heat and stir in pumpkin.

Chill until mixture mounds slightly when spooned. (Test every now and then, don't let it get too stiff.) Beat egg whites until soft peaks form; gradually add granulated sugar, beating to stiff peaks. Fold pumpkin mixture thoroughly into egg whites. Turn into cooled corn flake crust. Chill firm. Trim pie with a dollop of whipped cream and wreath of California walnut halves.

EXTRA RECIPES

Breads

BAKING TEMPERATURES AND TIMES

Food	Oven Temperature (°Fahrenheit)	Approximate Time Required for Baking (Minutes)
Quick Breads		
Biscuits	425° - 450°	10 - 15
Cream Puffs	450° then reduce to 350°	20-30, then 15-20
Popovers	450° then reduce to 350°	20-30, then 15-20
Muffins	400°	20 - 25
Loaves	350°	60 - 70
Coffee Cakes	350° - 375°	25 - 45
Yeast Breads		
Plain loaves	375° - 400°	30 - 45
Plain rolls	375° - 400°	10 - 20
Sweet rolls	375°	20 - 30

CONVERSION OF PAN AND UTENSIL SIZES TO METRIC MEASUREMENTS

Utensil	Metric Volume	Metric Measure in Centimetres	Closest Size in Inches or Volume
Baking or cake pan	2 L	20 cm square	8-inch square
	2.5 L	23 cm square	9-inch square
	3 L	30x20x5	12x8x2
	3.5 L	33x21x5	13x9x2
Cookie sheet		40x30	16x12
Jelly roll pan	2 L	40x25x2	15x10x¾
Loaf pan	1.5 L	20x10x7	8x4x3
	2 L	23x13x7	9x5x3
Round layer cake pan	1.2 L	20x4	8x1½
	1.5 L	23x4	9x1½
Pie Pan	750 mL	20x3	8x1¼
	1 L	23x3	9x1¼
Tube pan	2 L	20x7	8x3
	3 L	23x10	9x4
Spring form pan	2.5 L	23x6	9x3
	3 L	25x8	10x4
Baking dish	1 L		1 qt.
	1.5 L		1½ qt.
	2 L		2 qt.
	2.5 L		2½ qt.
	3 L		3 qt.
	4 L		4 qt.
Custard cup	200 mL		6 fl. oz.
Muffin pans	40 mL	4x2.5	1.5x1
	75 mL	5x3.5	2x1¼
	100 mL	7.5x3.5	3x1½
Mixing bowls	1 L		1 qt.
	2 L		2 qt.
	3 L		3 qt.

BREADS

CINNAMON BUNS
Gretchen Hopkins

20 frozen dough rolls
1 cup brown sugar
1/4 cup vanilla instant pudding

1 to 2 Tbsp cinnamon
3/4 cup raisins (optional)
1/4 to 1/2 cup melted butter

Grease a 10 inch bundt pan and add frozen rolls. Sprinkle with brown sugar, pudding powder, cinnamon and raisins. Pour melted butter over all. Cover with a clean, damp cloth. Let sit on the counter overnight. In the morning, preheat oven to 350°F and bake for 25 minutes. Let sit for 5 minutes and then turn out on a serving plate.

PATIO SNACK BREAD
Maureen Cockburn

2 cups grated cheddar cheese
1 cup sliced stuffed olives
1/3 cup melted butter
3 Tbsp chopped onion
1 egg, slightly beaten
1 1/2 cups all purpose flour

1 1/2 cups cornmeal
4 tsp baking powder
1 tsp salt
1 1/4 cups milk
1/3 cup vegetable oil

Combine the first five ingredients, mixing well. Set aside. Measure unsifted flour into mixing bowl. Add cornmeal, baking powder and salt; stir well to blend. Combine milk and oil and add all at once to flour mixture, mixing until soft dough is formed. Spread into a greased 10x15 inch pan. Spoon cheese-olive mixture over top. Spread evenly. Bake at 425°F for about 20 minutes. Yield: 2 dozen pieces.

*Wisdom consists of knowing
what to do with what you know.*

APPLE STREUSEL COFFEE CAKE

Alyson Clifton

2 1/4 cups flour
3/4 cup sugar
3/4 cup butter
1/2 tsp baking powder
1/2 tsp baking soda
1 egg, beaten

3/4 cup buttermilk or sour
  cream
1 can apple pie filling (cherry or
  blueberry filling can be
  substituted)
3/4 cup raisins (optional)

Preheat oven to 350°F. Grease a 9 inch springform pan. Combine flour and sugar. Cut in butter until crumbly. Set aside 1/2 cup of mixture. To remainder, add baking powder and soda. Combine egg and buttermilk (or sour cream) and add to dry ingredients, and stir until moistened. Spread 2/3 of batter over bottom of pan and part way up the sides.

Combine pie filling and raisins, if used, and spoon over batter. Drop spoonfuls of remaining batter over filling. Sprinkle with reserved crumb mixture. Bake for 50 to 55 minutes. Cherry or blueberry pie filling may be substituted.

SOUR CREAM COFFEE CAKE

Maureen Cockburn

First Mixture:
1/4 cup butter
1 cup sugar
2 eggs
1 cup sour cream
1 tsp baking soda
1 1/2 cups flour

1 1/2 tsp baking powder
1/4 tsp salt
Second Mixture:
1/2 cup brown sugar
1 1/2 tsp cinnamon
1/4 cup finely chopped nuts

Cream butter and sugar; beat in eggs. Stir and mix dry ingredients. Add to creamed mixture, alternating with sour cream. Mix well. Pour half of first mixture, in 10 inch angel food pan (or loaf pan). Sprinkle on half the second mixture. Add remaining first mixture and top with rest of second mixture. Bake at 350°F for 1 hour.

The only fool bigger than the person who knows it all is the person who argues with him.

BANANA BREAD

Gretchen Hopkins

3 ripe bananas
1 1/2 tsp baking soda
2 Tbsp milk
1/2 cup butter

1 cup sugar
1 beaten egg
1 1/2 cups flour

Mash bananas. Sprinkle soda over them and add milk. Mix butter, sugar and beaten egg in a separate bowl. Mix banana mixture together and add to butter mixture by folding. Fold in flour. Bake at 325°F for 55 minutes.

EASY & DELICIOUS BANANA BREAD

Alyson Clifton

1/4 cup butter
1 cup white sugar
1 egg

1 tsp baking soda
3 medium bananas, mashed
1 1/4 cups flour

Preheat oven to 350°F. Cream butter, gradually adding sugar. Add egg and beat well. Add bananas alternately with flour, mixing until fairly smooth. Pour into greased loaf pan. Bake for 45 to 60 minutes.

CASHEW CARROT LOAF

Jane Girard

6 cups chopped carrots
2 cups ground cashews
3 Tbsp oil
1 cup finely chopped leeks
1 cup finely chopped celery
1/2 cup whole wheat flour

1 tsp sea salt
1/2 tsp black pepper
2 tsp crushed sage
1/2 tsp thyme
1 tsp basil

Steam the carrots until tender, then mash them using a fork, potato-masher, blender or food processor. Six cups of chopped raw carrots make about 3 cups of mashed. Grind the cashews in a food processor or blender until they are quite fine. Add the oil to the blender, if necessary to help with the grinding. Mix all the ingredients together and place in an oiled loaf tin. Bake at 350°F for 35 to 45 minutes, or until the top edges begin to look dry.

Skipping classes will make the teacher hopping mad.

CRANBERRY BANANA LOAF

Amelia Coupland

1/4 cup melted butter
1 cup sugar
2 eggs
3/4 cup mashed bananas
1 cup whole cranberries (fresh
  or frozen)

1 1/2 cups flour
1 1/2 tsp baking powder
1/2 tsp baking soda
1/2 tsp cinnamon
1/2 tsp salt

Cream butter and sugar. Add eggs. Stir in cranberries and mashed banana. In another bowl mix remaining ingredients (flour, baking powder, baking soda, cinnamon and salt). Add all at once to the first mixture. Bake in greased loaf pan at 350°F for approximately one hour.

CRANBERRY ORANGE BREAD

Gretchen Hopkins

1/4 cup butter, softened
1 cup sugar
1 egg
1 tsp grated orange peel
2 cups all-purpose flour
1 tsp baking powder

1 tsp salt
1/2 tsp baking soda
3/4 cup orange juice
1 cup chopped fresh or frozen
  cranberries
1 cup golden raisins

In a large mixing bowl, cream butter and sugar. Beat in egg and orange peel. Combine the dry ingredients; add to creamed mixture alternately with juice. Fold in cranberries and raisins. Pour into a greased 9x5 inch loaf pan. Bake at 350°F for 60 to 65 minutes or until a toothpick inserted near the center comes out clean. Cool for 10 minutes; remove from pan to a wire rack to cool completely.

Experience is the name everybody
gives to their mistakes.

CHERRY LOAF

Maureen Cockburn

6 oz bottle maraschino cherries
2 cups sifted all purpose flour,
   divided
4 tsp baking powder
1/2 tsp salt

3/4 cup sugar
1/2 cup milk, plus (see method)
1 egg
3 Tbsp melted butter
1/2 cup walnuts

Preheat oven to 300°F. Drain cherry juice into measuring cup; add milk to bring liquid to 1 cup. Slice cherries and chop walnuts. Sift flour; take out 1/2 cup to flour cherries and nuts. Sift remaining flour with baking powder and salt. Beat egg; add sugar and beat until blended; stir in butter. Fold in fruit and nuts. Place in greased 8 1/4x4 1/4 inch loaf pan. Bake for 1 1/4 hours, or until well done.

ZUCCHINI NUT BREAD

Audrey Karpoff

2 cups shredded zucchini
3 eggs
1 cup vegetable oil
1 cup granulated sugar
1/3 cup molasses
2 tsp vanilla
2 cups all-purpose flour,
   unsifted

1/2 cup whole-wheat flour
1 tsp salt
1 tsp baking soda
1/2 tsp baking powder
2 tsp cinnamon
1 cup raisins
1 cup chopped nuts

Use the coarsest surface of a grater to shred the unpeeled zucchini. If zucchini is extremely watery, place it in a sieve to drain while preparing the batter.

In a large bowl of electric mixer, beat eggs to blend. Add oil, sugar, molasses and vanilla; continue beating until thick and foamy. Combine dry ingredients and add to the egg mixture. Stir just until blended. Add zucchini, raisins and nuts; mix gently to avoid further crushing the zucchini shreds. Divide and pour the batter into two 9x5 inch greased and floured loaf pans. Bake in 350°F oven for one hour or until the cake tests done. After cooled for about 10 minutes, remove from pans to finish cooling on racks. Makes 2 large loaves.

Character development is the true aim of education.

CHEDDAR & SUN-DRIED TOMATO BREAD   *Rita Bell*

1/4 cup finely chopped sun-dried tomatoes, packed in oil, or about 1/2 (6.5 oz) jar of sun-dried tomatoes, packed in oil
2 1/2 cups all-purpose flour
2 Tbsp granulated sugar
2 tsp baking powder
1/2 tsp each baking soda and salt
1 tsp dried rosemary
1 cup grated old cheddar cheese
1/4 cup thinly sliced green onions
2 Tbsp finely chopped parsley
1 egg
1 1/2 cups buttermilk
2 Tbsp each vegetable oil and oil drained from sun-dried tomatoes
1 crushed garlic clove

Preheat oven to 350°F. Generously grease a 9x5 inch loaf pan or coat with cooking spray. Remove about half of sun-dried tomatoes from the jar and chop finely. Measure flour, sugar, baking powder, baking soda and salt into a large mixing bowl. Measure out rosemary, crush or finely chop, and stir into flour mixture with grated cheese, onions and parsley. Make a well in center.

Beat egg in a small bowl. Add buttermilk, vegetable oil, oil from sun-dried tomatoes and garlic. Whisk together until blended. Pour into flour mixture and stir just until combined. Stir in sun-dried tomatoes until evenly distributed. Turn into greased pan. Smooth top. Bake in centre of oven until golden and a skewer inserted in the centre comes out almost clean, about 60 to 65 minutes. Immediately turn out of pan onto a cooling rack.

MUFFINS

BEST EVER BRAN MUFFINS   *Vi Sakaki*

1 cup margarine
2 cups brown sugar
2 Tbsp molasses
1/4 tsp salt
1 1/2 cups bran (natural)
2 3/4 cups flour
2 tsp baking powder
1 cup chopped walnuts
1 1/2 cups raisins
2 cups sour milk or buttermilk
2 tsp baking soda
2 beaten eggs

Cream margarine, brown sugar and molasses. Stir together salt, bran, flour, baking powder, nuts and raisins. Combine soda and sour milk. Add beaten eggs. Add dry mixture alternately with liquids to creamed mixture. Fill greased muffin tins 3/4 full. Bake at 375°F for 20 minutes. Yield: 30.

BRAN MUFFINS

Mary Krysko

- 4 cups (1 L) buttermilk or sour milk
- 4 cups natural bran
- 4 eggs
- 1 1/3 cups vegetable oil
- 4 tsp vanilla
- 1 1/3 cups brown sugar
- 1 cup white sugar
- 3 Tbsp molasses
- 4 tsp baking powder
- 4 tsp baking soda
- 4 cups flour
- 1/2 tsp salt
- 1 1/2 cups (or more) raisins
- Walnuts if desired

Mix buttermilk and natural bran together and soak until soft. In large mixing bowl beat eggs, then add vegetable oil, vanilla, brown sugar, white sugar, molasses and beat well. In another bowl, stir together dry ingredients. Add buttermilk mixture and flour mixture, alternating with egg mixture. Beat well. Add raisins and/or walnuts if desired and mix lightly. Place in muffin tins and bake in 350°F oven for 20 to 25 minutes. Makes 36 to 40 muffins. Freezes well.

YOGURT BRAN MUFFINS

Jackie Pawson

- 1 1/4 cups all-purpose flour
- 1 1/4 cups natural bran
- 3/4 cup packed brown sugar
- 1 Tbsp baking powder
- 1 tsp baking soda
- 1/4 tsp cinnamon
- 1/4 tsp salt
- 1 cup chopped dried apricots
- 1 cup low-fat yogurt
- 1/4 cup vegetable oil
- 1 egg
- 1 1/2 tsp vanilla

In bowl, combine flour, bran, sugar, baking powder, baking soda, cinnamon and salt. Reserve 2 tablespoons apricots; stir remaining apricots into bowl. Whisk together yogurt, oil, egg and vanilla. Stir into flour mixture just until combined. Spoon into lightly greased deep muffin tins, filling three-quarters full; press reserved apricots into tops. Bake in 375°F oven for 20 to 25 minutes or until golden and firm to the touch. Makes 12 muffins.

Just think how happy you'd be if you lost everything you have right now - and then got it all back again.

BLUEBERRY ORANGE MUFFINS

Sandy Taylor

1 3/4 cups all purpose flour
2/3 cup packed brown sugar
1 Tbsp baking powder
1 Tbsp grated orange rind
1 cup milk

3 eggs
3 Tbsp butter, melted
1 tsp vanilla
1 cup blueberries

In large bowl, combine flour, sugar, baking powder and orange rind. Whisk together milk, eggs, butter and vanilla; pour over dry ingredients. Sprinkle with blueberries; stirring just until dry ingredients are moistened. Spoon into greased muffin cups. Bake in 400°F oven for 20 to 25 minutes.

OATMEAL MUFFINS

Vi Sakaki

1 cup buttermilk
1 cup quick cooking rolled oats
1 egg
1/2 cup oil
1/2 cup brown sugar
1 cup flour
1 tsp baking powder

1/2 tsp baking soda
1/2 tsp cinnamon
1/2 tsp nutmeg
1/2 tsp salt
1/2 cup chopped dates
1/2 cup chopped walnuts

Mix buttermilk and quick cooking rolled oats together and let stand for 1 hour. Mix together egg, oil and brown sugar and add to buttermilk and rolled oats. Sift together dry ingredients and add to previous mixture, stirring until just blended. Add dates and walnuts and mix. Pour into greased muffin pans and bake in oven at 400°F for 15 to 20 minutes.

APPLE SAUCE OATMEAL MUFFINS

Sandy Taylor

1 cup flour
3 tsp baking powder
1/2 tsp cinnamon
1/2 tsp salt
1/4 tsp nutmeg
3/4 cup rolled oats

1/4 cup brown sugar
1 egg
1/4 cup vegetable oil
1/3 cup milk
2/3 cup apple sauce

Preheat oven to 400°F. Measure dry ingredients into a large bowl. Stir. Beat together egg, oil and milk. Stir in apple sauce. Do not over mix. Mix together. Bake for 15 minutes.

RHUBARB OATMEAL MUFFINS
Sandy Taylor

1/2 cup margarine
1 egg
1/2 tsp cinnamon
1/2 tsp baking soda
3/4 cup rhubarb sauce

3/4 cup brown sugar, packed
1 cup flour
1 tsp baking powder
1/4 tsp salt
1 cup rolled oats

Cream shortening and sugar. Beat in egg. Add dry ingredients to creamed mixture, alternating with rhubarb. Stir in oats last. Fill greased tins 3/4 full. Bake in 400°F oven for 15 minutes.

MISCELLANEOUS

POTATO PANCAKES
Jacqueline Fassnacht

1 lb potatoes, grated
1 small onion, grated
2 eggs
2 Tbsp chopped mint
1/4 cup crumbled feta cheese
1/4 cup all-purpose flour

Salt and freshly ground black
 pepper, to taste
4 Tbsp vegetable oil
Garnish with parsley, mint, and
 lemon wedges

Peel and grate the potatoes and onion. Stir in a little salt and place in a colander to drain for 15 to 20 minutes. Place the eggs in a bowl and beat lightly. Squeeze excess moisture from the potato mix and combine with the eggs, mint, feta, flour, and salt and pepper.

Heat the oil in a large non-stick frying pan. Add 2 tablespoons of mixture per pancake to the pan and squash to make flat 2 3/4 inch pancakes. Cook on both sides until golden brown. Serve garnished with fresh parsley and mint, and a wedge of lemon. Makes 8 to 10 pancakes.

*First you teach a child to talk; then
you have to teach it to be quiet.*

ZUCCHINI PANCAKES

Marilyn Kelm

1 1/2 cups unpeeled grated
 zucchini (press between
 paper towels to remove
 moisture)
2 Tbsp grated onion
1/4 cup Parmesan cheese

1/4 cup flour
2 eggs
2 Tbsp mayonnaise
1/4 tsp oregano
Salt and pepper, to taste

Mix ingredients together. Melt 1 tablespoon butter in skillet. Make pancakes using 2 tablespoons mixture for each. Flatten with spatula, brown both sides. Serve plain or top with tomato sauce. Add grated cheese or sour cream and chives. Serves 2 to 3.

MASHED POTATO PANCAKES

Sandy Taylor

2 cups mashed potatoes,
 cooled
1/2 cup tightly packed grated
 old cheddar
1/2 cup plain yogurt or sour
 cream

1 egg, slightly beaten
1/2 cup green onions, finely
 chopped
Pepper
Salt
Vegetable oil

In medium bowl, mix together mashed potatoes, cheese, yogurt, egg, green onions and a generous grinding of black pepper, until evenly mixed. Taste and add salt if needed. Using wet hands, form about 1/2 cup of mixture into a 2 1/2 inch round pancake. Place on waxed paper-lined tray. Repeat with remaining mixture. Heat over medium heat in just enough oil to coat the bottom of a large non-stick skillet. Add half of the pancakes, cook until golden brown on both sides and hot in the middle (3 to 4 minutes per side).

Children have never been good at listening to their elders, but they have never failed to imitate them.

YORKSHIRE PUDDING

Carole Woodward

3 large eggs
1 cup flour

1 cup 2% milk
1 tsp salt

Preheat oven to 450°F. Mix all ingredients together in bowl. No need to get rid of all the "lumps" so do not whip too much. Pour into greased large size muffin pans. Place pan on top shelf of oven and bake for about 20 minutes or until the puddings rise well. Serve immediately, traditionally with roast beef dinner, but Yorkshire pudding goes equally well with turkey, chicken, etc.

EXTRA RECIPES

138 MISCELLANEOUS

INDEX